Advance Praise for Vanessa Summers'
Get in the Game!
The Girls' Guide to Money and Investing

"Vanessa Summers has written **a breakthrough money guide for young women.** With humor and wisdom, she guides the reader through not only how but also why to save, invest, and put her own financial needs first. **She brings common sense and sophisticated insights** together in this elegantly written guide for young women of all ages."

Amy Domini
Founder
Domini Social Equity Fund

"*Get in the Game!* is indeed **a gift to all young women who are tired of being targeted by consumer marketing yet neglected when it comes to financial guidance.** As a young woman who has experienced the ugly truth of 'the more you make, the more you spend' and been able to defy that maxim by creating two businesses and a foundation by age thirty, I can assure that **this book is not only empowering—it also makes the money trail a lot less bumpy!**"

Christy Turlington
President of Nuala and Creative Director of Sundari

"**At last! A terrific financial book I can give my daughters** that they'll actually enjoy reading. It's cleverly written in their language using examples they can relate to. Vanessa Summers does a fabulous job of turning the complex subject of money into a simple, entertaining, and inspiring read. **If this doesn't spur the reader to action, I don't know what will!!** "

Barbara Stanny
Author of *Prince Charming Isn't Coming:
How Women Get Smart About Money*

Get
in the
Game!

Also of interest from
BLOOMBERG PRESS

Investing with Your Values:
Making Money and Making a Difference
Hal Brill, Jack A. Brill, and Cliff Feigenbaum

Investing in Small-Cap Stocks
Revised Edition
Chris Graja and Elizabeth Ungar, Ph.D.

Investing 101
Kathy Kristof

Plan Now or Pay Later:
Judge Jane's No-Nonsense Guide to Estate Planning
Jane B. Lucal

A Commonsense Guide to Your 401(k)
Mary Rowland

The New Commonsense Guide to Mutual Funds
Mary Rowland

Stock Options—Getting Your Share of the Action:
Negotiating Shares and Terms in Incentive
and Nonqualified Plans
Tom Taulli

A complete list of our titles is available at
www.Bloomberg.com/Books

Get in the Game!

the girls' guide to
money & investing

Vanessa Summers

BLOOMBERG PRESS

PRINCETON

Books are available for bulk purchases at special discounts. Special editions or book excerpts can also be created to specifications. For information, please write to: Special Markets Department, Bloomberg Press.

BLOOMBERG, BLOOMBERG NEWS, BLOOMBERG FINANCIAL MARKETS, OPEN BLOOMBERG, BLOOMBERG PERSONAL FINANCE, THE BLOOMBERG FORUM, COMPANY CONNECTION, COMPANY CONNEX, BLOOMBERG PRESS, BLOOMBERG PROFESSIONAL LIBRARY, BLOOMBERG PERSONAL BOOKSHELF, and BLOOMBERG SMALL BUSINESS are trademarks and service marks of Bloomberg L.P. All rights reserved.

First edition published 2001
1 3 5 7 9 10 8 6 4 2

Library of Congress Cataloging-in-Publication Data

Summers, Vanessa
    Get in the Game! : the girls' guide to money & investing / Vanessa Summers.
    p. cm.
    Includes index.
    ISBN 1-57660-096-3 (alk. paper)
      1. Young women—Finance, Personal. 2. Investments. I. Title.

  HG179 .S855 2001
  332.024'0084'22--dc21   2001035384

Acquired and edited by Kathleen A. Peterson

Produced and packaged by Book Laboratory Inc.,
Mill Valley, CA 94941

Book design and illustrations by Victoria Martin Pohlmann

This book is dedicated to my beautiful mother... and to all of the amazing spirits who have crossed my path offering love and sustenance, thus leaving footprints for a lifetime on my heart.

Heartfelt Thanks

... to all of the people who helped with this book. With love and gratitude to my family: my mother and father; my incredible little bros, Harry and Michael; and my gorgeous big sis, Michelle. Special thanks to Manuela Dunn for her unwavering support with this book, Rob Densen for being a great friend and mentor, and Rich Thau for being open and supportive about strategically working together to truly make a difference.

And for input, friendship, inspiration, kindness, laughter, and guidance, not necessarily in that order, thank you to my friends and colleagues: Teena Goulet, L. J. Carusone, Hall Powell, Stephanie Bowen, Mary Jo Wright, Larry Schultz, Jennifer Kushell, Ken Deckinger, Michael Zeppetello, Eliza and Hana Grizwold, Emily Thomas, Scott Elliot, Don Gable, Mimi Obadia, Kathy and Amy Eldon, John Quinn, Martine Jullien, Andy Stiles, Russell Jullius, Mr. Williams, and Allan Nichols.

This book is for all of the courageous young women out there who are open to learning how to conquer their own money trail through getting in the game—and even getting out of debt! I hope this book will help empower you to build the quality of life you want.

As a first-time author, with limited experience in the publishing world, I knew I was going to face several immediate challenges. However, my belief in thinking out of the box took this book, and my mind-set, to a new level, expanding the route of traditional book publishing. I chose to create the Sutra Foundation, a nonprofit organization that seeks to motivate, inspire, and teach young women to invest and plan for financial retirement—in effect, empowering young women through financial education. To help further the mission, I assigned all advances, royalties, and other payments earned on my behalf for writing *Get in the Game! The Girls' Guide to Money and Investing* as a donation to the foundation. Why a foundation? I wanted to make sure this book reached you through a call to action for all companies and individuals to work together with the foundation for a strategic sponsorship to help disseminate this book. Through creating the Sutra Foundation, I was able to set a tone of philanthropy for this book and to begin raising awareness that there truly is a market of young women (estimated twenty-three million in the United States ages eighteen to thirty-five) who need to be reached with a robust educational message about how to begin saving and investing.

I firmly believe that young women need strong messages from the marketplace, messages explaining why it is critical to start taking control of their money today. According to the Institute for Women's Policy Research, approximately 50 percent of all elderly (sixty-five and older) single/widowed women live on incomes of less than $12,000 per year. To make a difference as young women—to change our odds—we need the right information. That's where the Sutra Foundation—and this book—come in: *Get in the Game!* seeks to send a strong "how-to" educational message to young women about their money and how to invest it, all the while presented in a fun, hip, engaging manner. Better yet, the readers get the message from a peer!

I am incredibly thankful to my publisher, Bloomberg Press, and my editor Kathleen Peterson, for having the ability to see the urgent need for this book and for their unwavering enthusiasm in pioneering this project with the Sutra Foundation.

As young women, I believe we have a tremendous amount of opportunity, not only to be successful professionally but also to be powerfully creative about how we use our money. I hope my experiences and ideas will inspire your life the way your needs and desires have inspired mine to create this book. A gigantic "heartfelt thanks!" to all of the young women out there whose needs helped make my dream of writing this book a reality. Live with strength and joy, accept that each day is filled with wonderful change, and never forget that our lives are only limited by our imaginations. Life is your amazing adventure; where do you want to go?

Contents

Heartfelt Thanks . . . . **vii**

Introduction **1**

Chapter 1:
Welcome to the Adventure **7**

Chapter 2:
Value-Packed Goals **41**

Chapter 3:
Gear Up: Budget Lean and Debt Free **71**

Chapter 4:
Three Adventure Backpacks to Go, Please! **103**

Chapter 5:
Be a Trailblazer with Savvy Investment Gear **135**

Chapter 6:
Six Inspirational Summit Reserves **177**

Index **185**

Get in the Game!

Who the Heck Am I?
and why bother listening to Moi?

Hello! My name is Vanessa Summers, and I'm a twenty-nine-year-old x-tennis player, x-model, x-stockbroker, and x-employee of a women's fund. I'm also a registered investment advisor, and I want to help other young women understand how to take financial responsibility for themselves. I believe that young women are ambitious, independent, and strong—and that they want to get things right. If you take the time to read this guidebook, you will be giving yourself the opportunity to learn all of the basics about money and investing. In a nutshell, you will be giving yourself a chance to conquer the money trail!

Trust Me...

Not only am I a young woman, I'm a young woman who has been foolish with money. I understand what it's like to be in unfamiliar territory when it comes to personal financial planning (i.e., taking care of money). I entered the professional world as a seventeen-year-old fashion model in New York City.

During six years of international travel as a model, I never once understood the "time value" of money, what an interest rate was, or even if my current income would cover my monthly bills.

At twenty-three, I had the opportunity to pursue a career in Hong Kong as a stockbroker with a top investment bank. I spent four years there learning about fundamental analysis, the global economic system, and stock market investing. Not once, however, did I apply that knowledge to my personal financial life.

I didn't understand how to save for retirement, how to put myself first, or even how to set a budget (and secretly, in the back of my mind, I believed that someday I would end up marrying someone wealthy).

Upon returning to the United States, I humbly claimed ten years of business experience, ten years during which I was never in control of my financial journey. There I was, making so much money, and I never even knew how to **"get in the game"** and summit my own money trail.

The Other Side

In the spring of 1998, soon after my return from Asia, I was introduced to the concept of socially responsible investing. I took a position as head of sales and marketing at a women's fund and quickly learned the critical steps I needed to take to ascend my own money trail. Once I consciously sought to initiate my hike on the money trail, my job, friendships, dating, where I lived, how I saw myself, and even what I thought I was capable of changed in a powerfully positive way. In no time at all my self-esteem and sense of self-worth began to quietly shift. It was as if I had suddenly turned on the light in a dark room, a room where my personal finances, alone and unkempt, had sat collecting dust. I now understand that up until that point, I unknowingly *chose* not to deal with my personal finances. Keeping this important part of my life in the dark affected every aspect of my life and how I chose to live it. I had been hiking the money trail all along, but had no idea I was even on it!

Now that I know I'm on the money trail and have taken the time to learn personal financial responsibility, I feel available to build and live the life I truly want on all levels. By knowing exactly where I stand on my money scale and what direction I'm heading to summit my money trail, I'm able to take greater risks and open myself up to achieving more than I ever thought I was capable of, like writing this book for you! I've learned that if I don't give myself the power to improve, I'm leaving the fate of my happiness in somebody else's hands.

By allowing myself to be an adventurer on the money trail, I'm empowering my chances for a healthy, happy, fulfilled life that has an ending with no regrets. For the first time ever I feel in control of my life—and that is a very good thing.

> "We know what we are,
> but know not what we may be."
> **—William Shakespeare**

Summiting the Money Trail

The reality is, we all deal with money each day. In effect, we are all hiking the money trail! The question is, "Does how you deal with your money work for you?" I believe that we, as young women, are completely capable of taking charge of our finances and financial futures. All that's required is that we be given the right information to get started. In this book I'm going to equip you with the tools you will need to successfully deal with your money. As your guide, I will show you how to summit the money trail that in return will empower you to deal with your money confidently and successfully!

In Chapter 1 I will show you key facts and figures that explain the challenges all women face and the importance of starting your journey now. I will also explain to you key checkpoints on the money trail and why it is critical for young women to start investing early—charts and graphs will illustrate the financial reality we all face whether we want to admit it or not. In conclusion, I will show you how to begin organizing your financial materials.

In Chapter 2 you will learn that before hitting the money trail you need to equip yourself with what I call "values tools." Successful financial planning begins with your values. Once you identify these, you will learn how to set goals that will enable you to live your dreams as a carefree hiker on the money trail.

In Chapter 3 you will be able to quickly evaluate where you stand today on the money scale. I will show you shortcuts for making your money go the distance and how to hike your steep pitch free of debt. You may also choose to go a step further and learn more about your debt, whether from credit cards, student loans, or something else.

In Chapter 4 you will learn how to map out a financial life filled with health, wealth, and good fun through learning how you can build three "adventure backpacks:" one for emergencies, another for retirement, and a third for dreams. This chapter includes helpful hints on tax-free retirement options, plus important information on why you absolutely need disability insurance.

In Chapter 5 I will show you how you can be a trailblazer by choosing savvy investment gear that will help you get the most out of your money. You will learn how to confidently identify the best gear for you while taking in both the short and long views on the money trail.

Finally, in Chapter 6, I will leave you with six "inspirational summit reserves." These uplifting remarks will encourage you to start your money adventure today!

Remember to use this book with my voice as your guide, because you are about to embark on...

a journey that will change your life!

"What you already know
is merely a good departure point."
—Keorapetse Kgositsile

chapter 1

Welcome to the Adventure

"Our deepest fear is not that we are inadequate. Our deepest fear is that we are powerful beyond measure."
—**Nelson Mandela**

Congratulations, you made it! By picking up this book, you just took a very important step toward achieving financial security and independence. You've made a great decision, one that will provide you with an unlimited amount of self-esteem and freedom.

This book aims to motivate and inspire young women to organize their finances, discipline their spending, and begin to invest successfully, the objective being empowerment through education about money with a focus on value-based investing for emergencies, retirement, and fulfilling your dreams. Taking control of your finances as a young woman means giving yourself control of your life in the here and now. After reading this book you will live your life comfortably and confidently, knowing you are capable of taking care of you.

In this chapter you will learn why it is imperative that you begin taking control of your finances now. The reality is that we are all hiking the money trail each and every day with the many different decisions we make. We need to be conscious of being on the money trail and proactive in how we will summit it in this lifetime.

I remember when I thought taking control of my money would be a complicated, lengthy process. I felt intimidated. In reality, what I needed to learn was all very simple and basic stuff. At our age we don't actually need much to amass great wealth. Two of the key tools I will show you available to us are time and compound interest. I will explain how to easily give yourself an extra fifty bucks a month without getting a raise and what investing that small amount can do for you over the next thirty to forty years. Have you ever heard the saying "The hardest part of the journey is just showing up for the ride?" Well, you've already done that by choosing to read this book. Way to go!

And by the way, your timing is fantastic. There's never been a better time for women, particularly those our age, to map out their financial futures. Take a look at these exciting statistics:

Working women currently earn more than **$1 trillion** every year, and over 300,000 women have incomes of more than **$100,000**. (U.S. Bureau of Labor Statistics)

There are **58 million women** in the current workforce, and that number is growing faster than the male component of the workforce. (U.S. Department of Labor)

> As of 1999, there were **9.1 million** women-owned businesses in the United States employing over 27.5 million people and generating over **$3.6 trillion** in sales. (National Foundation for Women Business Owners)

> Between 1987 and 1999, the number of women-owned firms increased by **103 percent** nationwide. (National Foundation for Women Business Owners)

> As of 1999, women-owned firms accounted for **38 percent** of all firms in the United States. It is expected that within the next few years, women will own a majority of the nation's small businesses. (National Foundation for Women Business Owners)

> Thanks in part to the accessibility of the World Wide Web, women are founding companies at **twice** the rate of men. (National Foundation for Women Business Owners)

Got to Hit the Money Trail

These statistics are great news for women in general, but when it comes to our personal finances, the picture isn't so pretty. Because the choices we make as young women are heavily influenced by our financial situation, it's important to pay special attention to our personal money matters.

In this book I will show you how to positively evaluate and assess your financial situation according to your money values and goals. Identifying your money values means that you understand what is most meaningful to you about money, for example, security, flexibility, power, or even time. It's critical to know your money values, because they will guide your financial choices, choices that will ultimately reflect the life you choose to build. Equipping yourself with your values tools will enable you to set personal goals that reflect those values.

Where you choose to live, what car you drive, your vacation plans, and how often you eat out are circumstances unique to you. As we grow older the money question becomes broader, seeping into every aspect of our lives. What sort of home will we be able to afford? Where will our children be educated? Will we be able to care for our aging parents? Will we be able to retire young enough to still enjoy retirement? Absorb from this book what you and your financial life thirst for, which may be everything.

As "young-gals," we are lucky to have the best opportunity to build the life we dream of. I wrote this book because I want you to succeed in getting all that you want!

> "To improve the golden moment of opportunity, and catch the good that is within our reach, is the great art of life."
> —**Samuel Johnson**

The Statistics Don't Lie

I remember speaking at a conference a while back that was focused on educating women about money. It was one of my first public speaking engagements, and I was completely absorbed in my own world of nervousness about my speech on socially responsible investing.

As I waited my turn at the podium, I began to hear the song "Money, Money, Money" belting over the loudspeaker. Eight hundred plus baby boomer women stood up in the conference room with great excitement as this big, beautiful woman took the stage. I don't recall her name, but I remember her shocking words with clarity. The latest statistics on the personal financial condition of women in this country silenced the room. You could feel a sincere sense of sadness overtake the energy of the audience. I felt completely numb to learn that 50 percent of elderly single/widowed women in this country live on incomes of $1,000 dollars or less a month. In effect, these women are poor! *How could this be?* I thought. I knew I was lucky, but after hearing what the speaker before me had to say, I wasn't feeling so lucky. For the first time I began to consider the "what-ifs" of my financial future. What was going to keep me from becoming one of those elderly poor women myself one day? Since I hadn't done any personal financial planning myself, I knew the answer was *nothing*.

In hindsight, this woman's speech was my wake-up call, and the statistics were my awakening to the truth about my financial future. A sense of reality began to set in to such a degree that I wouldn't know the extent of it for several months.

The truth was that no one other than me was going to take control of my financial future. You will find in the next few paragraphs the same statistics that were shared with me. This is *your* time to absorb the information and use your newfound knowledge as a springboard to take control of your financial destiny.

Remember, you are already on the road to a happier, healthier, and more promising financial future. You can do this ...

just keep reading!

For women, the ride to financial security has been long, bumpy, and scary for many reasons, including the fact that women have longer life spans than men. According to the National Council of Women's Organizations,

women live an average of seven years longer than men.

It is estimated that half of women older than sixty-five outlive their husbands by fifteen years. What is even more depressing is the average age of widowhood, currently fifty-six.

A girlfriend of mine had a grandmother who turned sixty-five back in 1990. She was one of those sweet, doting grandmothers who would always have a fresh batch of chocolate chip cookies waiting for you upon your arrival. Unfortunately, her husband passed away in 1988, and my girlfriend's grandmother had to move out of her beautiful three-bedroom home and into a state-run nursing home. As a young woman growing up in the first half of the 1900s, she said that she was not taught anything about money, except to find a good husband who would take care of her for the rest of her life. In reality, her husband took care of her for the rest of *his* life.

Another problem we face as women is the fact that women typically earn less than men. According to the Women's Institute for a Secure Retirement,

women typically earn $.72 for every $1 earned by men.

That means women earn on average only 72 percent of what men earn, which equals a lifetime loss of over $250,000. As women, we have a greater chance of being affected by corporate downsizing. We are also less likely to have a steady income stream over a long period of time, partly due to responsibilities involving child rearing and the care of elderly parents. In fact, the National Council of Women's Organizations reports that 21 percent of women between the ages of twenty-five and forty were not employed in 1996, compared to only 7 percent of men. Many of these women are mothers of young children.

As a result of all these circumstances, we, just by the mere fact of being women, accumulate less money toward our retirement savings, which means our accumulated retirement benefits are going to be lower.

It is estimated that approximately 50 percent of men receive retirement benefits, while only about one in five women receive retirement benefits, a shocking 20 percent of all women. And as noted earlier, according to the Institute for Women's Policy Research, approximately 50 percent of all elderly (sixty-five and older) single/widowed women live on incomes of less than $12,000 per year. Think this is bad? Well, sorry, girls—it just got worse. According to the U.S. Commerce Department's Census Bureau, nearly half (45 percent) of women sixty-five and older are widowed. Of the elderly widows, seven in ten live alone. Imagine half of your girlfriends, or even you, alone and broke in the years to come. Doesn't sound like a whole lotta fun to *moi*. But that's why you're reading this...

**Time to take charge of
how fit you will be to hike the long
money trail ahead of you!**

Challenge 1:
You're trekking solo on
the money trail.

A major hurdle to overcome is the idea that a man is going to take care of your finances.

First of all, if men are so good at handling the family financial planning, why is it that only 5 percent of American families can afford to retire at age sixty-five?

In actuality, only 5 percent of Americans age sixty-five and over have annual incomes in excess of $25,000, not much to retire with. And, of course, the numbers for women are even worse. The average income for a sixty-five-year-old woman is less than $7,000 a year.

As for divorce, women are again on a slippery slope. If you thought you were going to marry a wealthy man and life would work out swimmingly, I have a rude little awakening for you. Divorce rates are now running as high as 50–54 percent for new marriages.

DIVORCE RATES IN THE UNITED STATES, 1920–2000

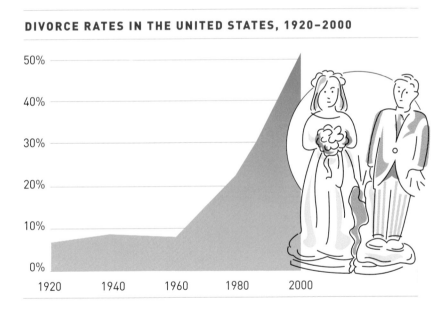

What's more depressing is that for more than 50 percent of these women, a second marriage will also end in divorce. In fact, not only do second marriages have a greater failure rate, but they tend to be shorter as well. Taking that a step further, it has been estimated that a man's quality of life will improve by a dramatic 35 percent postdivorce, while ours will decrease by an estimated 30 percent. There's only one slightly upbeat piece of news I've found on divorce for women. According to a 1989 survey conducted by the National Center for Women and Retirement Research on midlife women (those approximately forty years old) divorcing, more than half of the divorced women in the survey said that sex became more pleasurable two years postdivorce… just in case you were wondering!

TRAIL TALE…

I have firsthand experience of growing up in a family that was part of that second statistic, a man's postdivorce quality of life increasing while a woman's decreases. My mother married my stepfather when I was five. My mother, stepfather, older sister, and I lived happily together for more than ten years. My mother was among the first group of women in the United States to get her M.B.A. in the late 1970s. Instead of putting that degree to use, however, she fulfilled my stepfather's wishes with the birth of my two half brothers. To my dismay, my mother divorced my stepfather when I was seventeen, and we went bankrupt due to a poor investment choice my stepfather had made earlier that year.

At forty-two years of age, with two young boys to raise, my mother entered the workforce as a retail broker for Merrill Lynch. Watching my mother study for her Series 7 brokerage license with her twenty-two- to twenty-six-year-old colleagues in the Merrill Lynch training program was interesting.

Thanks to hard work and diligence, my mother has built a small nest egg for herself. However, after divorcing my step-father, she was forced to sell the house where I grew up, a house with six bedrooms, four baths, a pool, and a cabana on one acre of land. My mother left the country club lifestyle for a small condominium in the Midwest.

My mother's struggle to raise two small boys on her own with a full-time job has greatly affected my outlook on life. I find myself living with the subconscious fear that I can't count on a man, even though at times I continue to test the waters.

Besides, even if you happen to beat the one in two odds against divorce, what if you outlive your partner? Will you know what order the estate is in? Many women who escape the wrong end of the divorce statistic are not so lucky when they lose their spouse and their entire estate due to poor financial planning on their husband's part. Not only are these women left grieving, but they are also left financially destitute at a time when they most need help. These women are not alone. According to the U.S. Commerce Department's Census Bureau,

**nearly four times as many widows
live in poverty
as wives of the same age.**

The inescapable truth is that there is a good percentage chance you are going to outlive a partner and earn less than he does over the span of your professional career. Should you choose to marry, the financial situation doesn't look any brighter, what with divorce and widowhood.

Why leave your life to chance when you can equip yourself with the tools you need to hit the money trail now? I hope that you're not letting this information scare you too much but that you're getting ready to deal with it. You can do this! I've taken great care to keep this book fun, engaging, and simple. What you will learn on this special journey with me will give you the courage to take the right steps for yourself and your future. It's time to seize the day, girls!

Challenge 2:
Social Security blues!

You may be asking yourself, "What about Social Security?" You know, the money that's automatically deducted from your paycheck every month? You shouldn't discount Social Security as a supplemental option to retirement income, but you definitely shouldn't rely completely on these benefits. Why? The Social Security Administration caps the limit you can draw from the system. The current maximum any retired person can collect from benefits as of year 2000 is $1,433 a month, which comes out to a measly $17,196 a year. That means that no matter how much you put into the system over a lifetime, the maximum you're going to get is a little over seventeen grand a year! Plus, for women it looks even worse. The National Center for Women and Retirement Research reports that even with Social Security, the median annual income of women over sixty-five is $7,300. You don't need me to tell you that that ain't enough!

Yes, that's a happy thought isn't it? Here we are as young women, having all this money automatically deducted from our hard-earned monthly paycheck to go toward Social Security, and we probably won't see much or any of it.

Any of it? For starters, Social Security may not be around when we're set to retire. The Social Security Administration currently predicts that by the year 2013 the system will be paying out more than it's taking in, and unless Congress finds the money for a complete overhaul, there won't be enough money in the fund to pay out full benefits. According to a September 1994 survey sponsored by Third Millennium, a national nonprofit organization launched by young adults whose goals include promoting sustainable reform of Social Security and Medicare, more adults

---

Your Social Security Account

You can call Social Security at 800-772-1213 and make a request for your Personal Earnings and Benefit Statement free of cost, which you should receive automatically three months before your birthday if you are twenty-five years or older. If you have access to the Internet you can request one from the Social Security Administration's Web site at www.ssa.gov/. This statement will show your Social Security earnings history, estimate your future benefits, and earned credits.

Social Security will also give you an estimate of the disability benefits you could receive if you become severely disabled before you're eligible for full retirement. It is possible for a young person who has worked and paid Social Security taxes for as few as eighteen months to become eligible for disability benefits. Social Security is portable and will move with you from job to job throughout your career. One other thing to note, if you were born after the year 1960, you will not be able to draw Social Security benefits until you are sixty-seven, as opposed to the current age of sixty-five for retirees.

ages eighteen to thirty-four believe UFOs exist than believe Social Security will exist by the time they retire (46 percent compared to 28 percent).

Are you getting the picture? Even if the Social Security system is still around when you retire, the amount you can draw from the plan is capped at an extremely low threshold given the predicted cost of living, even as a retiree!

Challenge 3:
Use your imagination when it comes to inflation.

You read correctly, use your imagination when it comes to inflation. Inflation is what keeps you from hiking one of those steep pitches on the money trail. Inflation is the percentage increase of the prices on all goods and services in the economy. On average, the annual increase has been 5 percent in the last ten years and 3.5 percent in the last twenty years.

This means you can count on roughly a 4 percent increase per annum going forward. But the most important fact to remember when it comes to inflation is that your money will need to grow at a faster rate than inflation just so you don't lose money each year. This is why you need to make sure that your employer is offering you at least a 5 percent pay increase each year. I know that 4 percent may not sound like much to you, but take a look at this chart and see for yourself what inflation does over a long period of time.

HISTORICAL AND PROJECTED CONSUMER PRICES

Typical Prices	house	automobile	gasoline (10 gallons)	stamp
1950	$ 19,747	$ 3,400	$ 1.80	$ 0.03
1980	$ 67,517	$ 12,093	$ 6.16	$ 0.15
2000	$ 133,300	$ 25,140	$ 15.50	$ 0.33
2020 (Projection)	$521,383	$ 101,198	$ 34.65	$ 1.19

Sources: National Association of Realtors, National Association of Automobile Dealers, United States Post Office

As you can see, the future terrain on the money trail is going to cost you big-time! Have you ever heard your parents say, "When I was your age, I bought a house for what your car costs?" No kidding, the future is not going to be cheap, a perfect reason to begin conquering the money trail now.

For those of you who don't think this applies to you because you have plenty of money in a savings account, think again. Savings account rates at most banks are currently running at 0 to 1.5 percent. Yes, that's right. You read the appalling rate of interest correctly. We women traditionally like to keep a portion of our nest egg quietly tucked away, but these savings accounts are doing more harm than good. You won't beat inflation this way, and you won't beat the market. I will visit this entire subject more thoroughly in Chapter 3. For now, please note, you cannot count on building any real asset ascension with a savings account.

One last thing: for retirees inflation is a real killer. Retirement is something you probably haven't even thought of, but it's unavoidable. In fact, retirement is where most women run into trouble. Most people retire on fixed incomes. That means if inflation is growing at 4 percent a year, your purchasing power will be cut nearly in half in fifteen years.

Simply put, the dollar sitting in your wallet will only be worth about fifty cents a decade and a half from now. Ugh! Did someone say the government had inflation under control? No need to be discouraged. If you can discipline yourself to finish this book, you're beating it already.

Now that you know why it's important to hit the money trail, don't tell yourself that you're not qualified. Don't think that because you don't have tons of extra cash you can't succeed at investing.

Summit Checkpoint 1: Bigger Paychecks ≠ More Wealth

One of the great illusions about wealth is that you can get rich by making more money. But for most of us, making more money means only one thing: spending more money. We would be lucky, at our age, to learn this lesson now. Some of us have watched our parents and our parents' friends become disillusioned too late in life to start over.

The good news, girls, is you're different. You've already set yourself apart from the mainstream. At one point, as you continue to read, something is going to click. For you, doors are going to open that you never even knew existed. You're doing great!

> "The ability to simplify means to eliminate the unnecessary so that the necessary may speak."
> —**Hans Hoffman**

Stop the Cycle

You've probably had the experience of getting your first job. Now that you work part-time or full-time, you get a regular paycheck. Let's assume that once you got your job, you rented an apartment, leased a car, bought new clothes for work, and bam! You were tapped out. Then, a year or two down the road, suppose you got a raise. What did you do with that hard-earned money? You were on to the bigger apartment, the newer car, and the nicer clothes.

Americans Are Wonderful Consumers

This means that the more we make, the more we spend. Want proof? The stock market index known as the Nasdaq (National Association of Securities Dealers Automated Quotation System) climbed an aggressive 48 percent in the quarter immediately preceding the 1Q2000 (meaning first quarter in the year 2000). Take a look at the following chart.

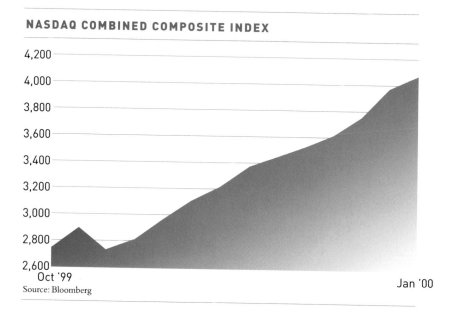

NASDAQ COMBINED COMPOSITE INDEX

4,200

4,000

3,800

3,600

3,400

3,200

3,000

2,800

2,600

Oct '99

Source: Bloomberg

Jan '00

Economic expansion expectations in the United States were strong, and Americans couldn't get enough of all the latest technology and dot-com stocks. Interestingly, the Bureau of Economic Analysis recorded in their "Overview of the Economy" report that personal consumption expenditures in the U.S. economy correspondingly jumped a hefty 30 percent, from $5.9 billion to $7.6 billion from 4Q99 (meaning fourth quarter in the year 1999) to the 1Q2000, once again proving that

the more we make, the more we spend!

And the more money we make, the more we raise our standards of living. If you don't keep track of your spending, your spending keeps track of you. Will your spending come back to haunt you when you're trying to retire? It's a distant thought, I know, but it's worth considering.

Are you a high roller? Do you work long hours at least five days a week to get a paycheck? If you don't hang on to some of that hard-earned money, what will you have to show for it further down the money trail? *Alone, Poor, and Aging* is not the guidebook I'm writing for you, thank you very much.

TRAIL TALE...

When I was twenty-three, I went to Hong Kong to seek my fortune as a stockbroker. I was under the impression that if I wanted to be wealthy, I had to make the mucho bucks. Unfortunately, in all of my travels up to that point, I never learned that to accumulate real wealth I needed to spend less and keep more. Let's think about this for a second. When it comes to consumerism, young women are one of the biggest media targets. We are continually bombarded by messages to spend, spend, spend, through the fashion magazines we read, television ads, and even the World Wide Web. With everyone in the media sending us the very opposite message, it's no wonder we're completely uncomfortable with saving and investing.

After always spending more than I made in Hong Kong, I was astonished upon returning to the United States to learn the lesson of spending less to keep more. Surprisingly, when I equipped myself with the financial tools I needed to summit my own money trail, it hit home hard. As I pondered my Hong Kong purchase of $2,000 worth of Louis Vuitton luggage, I knew that I had been made a fool. The more I thought about it, the more I realized that when we make more money, we spend more money, and it's usually not as an investment. And of course there are those of us who continue to spend more even without making more. For many of us, all of this consumption merely leads to more debt and more stress. The bigger the pay-check, the higher the standard of living. I reiterate, nobody is getting rich in this equation. The key concept here is not how much you make, but

how much do you keep?

Instead of waiting for that six-figure salary, or even if you have one now, it's time to start making the most out of what you have. Later in this book I will show you simple, strong, powerful strategies to help you build your

1. emergency adventure backpack
2. retirement adventure backpack
3. dream adventure backpack

You're on your way to a better hike on the money trail if you keep more of what you make!

This is great news, girls! You don't have to pull in a fat paycheck to make this system work for you. All you have to have is courage. It's easy and simple to apply the different concepts in this book today. No joke, you will be in a better place than you were when you started.

> "Most people see what is,
> and never see what can be."
> —**Albert Einstein**

For the skeptics out there who truly believe their problem lies with their income stream, take a look at the chart on the following page to see the amount of money that will pass through your hands in your lifetime. Try to imagine the amount of wealth you could amass if you could find a way to keep the money you make, or at least a good portion of it.

What do you currently make a month? How much money will you make over the course of your professional life? It's probably *more* than six figures. Don't you think you deserve to keep some of that money? I do. And yes, I understand that retail therapy is very real and very powerful to us women. However, learning to lasso that wild mustang spending will have a much longer, more gratifying and profound impact on how you feel about yourself, your life, and your adventurous journey.

The truth is that most Americans work ninety thousand hours in one lifetime, earning between $1 million and $3 million. The problem is we have nothing to show for it. At what point do we separate ourselves from "most Americans" to become millionaires?

EARNINGS OUTLOOK PROJECTIONS

Monthly Income	10 Years	20 Years	30 Years	40 Years
$1,000	$120,000	$240,000	$360,000	$480,000
$2,000	$240,000	$480,000	$720,000	$960,000
$3,000	$360,000	$720,000	$1,080,000	$1,440,000
$4,000	$480,000	$960,000	$1,440,000	$1,920,000
$5,000	$600,000	$1,200,000	$1,800,000	$2,400,000
$6,000	$720,000	$1,440,000	$2,160,000	$2,880,000
$7,000	$840,000	$1,680,000	$2,520,000	$3,360,000
$8,000	$960,000	$1,920,000	$2,880,000	$3,840,000
$9,000	$1,080,000	$2,160,000	$3,240,000	$4,320,000
$10,000	$1,200,000	$2,400,000	$3,600,000	$4,800,000

Learn to Spend Like a True Millionaire

> "A man's greatness is measured not by the things he has but by the things he can do without."
> —**Henry David Thoreau**

Coincidentally, the first month I returned to the United States from Hong Kong, I picked up a copy of Tom Stanley's *The Millionaire Next Door*. Basically, Stanley's book is about putting up a front vs. being real. One would assume that people with Porsches and four-story homes have millions of dollars of cash in the bank and no credit card debt, but I knew two wealthy families growing up in Florida that ended up bankrupt after living in mansion-style settings. Unfortunately, one of them happened to be my family.

I can't even count the number of rock-and-roll stars who started building multimillion dollar homes in California but never finished because their albums stopped selling. Does VH1's "Behind the Music—MC Hammer" ring a bell? Everyone just assumes these people have oodles of cash locked up in CDs and bonds (we will further discuss these types of investments in Chapter 5) for a rainy day. The biggest spenders act like they have money coming out their ears.

Stanley proves otherwise. Actually, nine times out of ten, these people with the beautiful façades are in debt over their heads. Real millionaires have a net worth of $3.7 million and live in a house worth $320,000. Half of the millionaires interviewed in Stanley's book never paid more than $399 for a suit. But here's the point I want you to take from Stanley's book:

Millionaires are dedicated investors!

On average, millionaires invest nearly 20 percent of their total household income each year—that's $26,200 a year they could be spending on cars and vacations. But the catch is, they don't. The millionaires in Stanley's book describe themselves as "tightwads" who think that charity starts at home.

Take heart. Spending less doesn't mean there will be no shopping; it just means guilt and self-loathing won't be involved. I'm going to show you how to be budget lean and debt free on your money trail without starving you from much-needed retail therapy shopping excursions! Remember, keep your heart and mind open. You are a strong and confident woman. You can do this; I know you can!

Summit Checkpoint 2: You have all the equipment you need right under your nose.

> "Do what you can, with what you have, where you are."
> —**Theodore Roosevelt**

For us, as young women, investing is not a priority. Most of us live month to month, paycheck to paycheck. We tell ourselves that we don't have enough money to be an investor or even to think of addressing our financial situation.

We are so overwhelmed, juggling so many new responsibilities and roles, that we honestly believe there is no way we can tackle investing right now. We leave the entire financial-planning topic alone, not knowing what lies ahead. There are also those of us who have the time and money but just don't *feel* like addressing it. It's not that we're lazy or unappreciative. We realize we have opportunities our mothers never did. We know that we're seeking financial independence. We're ambitious and strong.

We continue to ask ourselves the same questions: How do I balance my work and social life? How can I make it to the gym this week? Am I getting enough rest and sleep to function properly? How will I make my car payment and still afford to pay off my student loans this month? When will I be able to afford a vacation?

We're concerned about our survival and success on the money trail in one form or another whether we realize it or not. As we struggle to establish ourselves and our self-worth, personal finances play a key role. We subconsciously believe that learning to invest would be too much at this point in our busy lives. Most of us would rather put off investing until we are in our late thirties. But why do this when you already have all the financial equipment you need to get started?

Right Under Your Nose

With very little money up front you can grow a strong foundation. Over time, even with a small amount, you can actually build a sizable portfolio of assets. Start right here, right now. Read this sentence, the money trail mantra, three times, or until it is absorbed into your brain:

> **You can be a successful investor, and you can plan for your future.**

This is the foundation you need to lay before hitting the money trail. Lay it now!

Simply by reading this book you are creating the basis for a self-fulfilling prophecy. You *will* get your finances under control. You *will* have enough emergency money. You *will* be able to retire comfortably, because you'll be making your money work for you. You *will* have the freedom to live your dreams.

The Latte Factor

First, however, you need to understand the power of the "latte factor." The *latte factor* is an old stockbroker term used to help the broker's clients evaluate their spending by asking, "How much money do you spend on coffee a day?"

To keep this simple, let's say you are twenty-five and spend $2.50. If you take that $2.50 and save it each day instead of buying a coffee, in one month you will have $50. With only $50 a month, or even less, you can become an investor, putting yourself on the road to financial security.

This is only one example to help you understand the power of investing. But don't panic that you've frittered away hundreds of dollars on lattes, or Chinese takeout, or whatever. As a young woman, you have something incredibly powerful on your side: time.

The earlier you start saving, the better!

With only $50 a month, you will be able to invest $600 a year. If you put that $600 into a retirement plan through your employer, it could grow tax free until you retire. Stocks have held an average growth rate of 12 percent over the last fifty years. If you buy $600 worth of stock every year until you retire, there is a good chance you will have more than $500,000 by the time you've reached sixty-five. Not sure this all makes sense? Take a look at the chart below.

HOW MUCH YOU NEED TO INVEST TO MAKE A MILLION BUCKS
12% Annual Interest Rate*

Starting Age	Daily Savings	Monthly Savings	Yearly Savings
20	$2.00	$61	$730
25	$3.57	$109	$1,304
30	$6.35	$193	$2,317
35	$11.35	$345	$4,144
36	$12.77	$388	$4,660
37	$14.37	$437	$5,244
38	$16.18	$492	$5,904
39	$18.22	$554	$6,652
40	$20.55	$625	$7,500

*Please make note that regular deposits are required to amass $1 million by the age of 65 at the 12% stated rate of return.

Notice in the chart above that a twenty-five-year-old only needs to save $109 a month, or $1,304 a year, to accumulate a million bucks by retirement, whereas a thirty-five-year-old will need to save $345 a month, or $4,144 a year, to get to a million bucks by age sixty-five (ouch!). How about a forty-year-old? Even worse, a forty-year-old woman will need $625 a month, or $7,500 a year, to retire a millionaire at age sixty-five.

Trekking Right Along

I hope the message is becoming clear. Now you know why it's important to hit the money trail now: the statistics are not on our side. And you know that you're qualified and equipped to conquer the money trail because you have the resources. You don't need a six-figure salary to start investing, nor do you need to stop shopping. I hope you're psyched about this whole money journey. Let's begin!

Getting Your Act Together

What you need to do now is gather all of the important information, documents, and receipts listed below. Do not skip this step. It will help you assess your current financial situation. You will need eleven files to complete this first assignment, so go to it, girl! Feel free to check off the list as you complete each item (this is the audience-participation part!).

1. Get all of your checking and savings account statements together. Put them in a file labeled "Checking and Savings Information."

2. Get all of those yucky credit card statements and put them in a file labeled "Credit Card Debt Information."

3. Get any/all information you have regarding your Social Security benefits and put them in a file labeled "Social Security Information."

4. Gather all of your monthly bills (phone, electric, cable TV, cell phone) and put them in a file labeled "Utilities Information."

5. Get all of your insurance documents (including health, car, and disability) and put them in a file labeled "Insurance Information."

6. If you have a home mortgage, gather all statements and put them in a file labeled "Home Mortgage Information." If you rent, put your lease in a file labeled "Apartment Lease Information."

7. Gather any records concerning any other debts you may have, for example, car loans and student loans. Put them in a file labeled "Liabilities Information" or file them separately. (FYI, *liabilities* is another word for "debt.")

8. Gather all receipts year to date. Put them in a file labeled "Current Year Receipts Information."

9. Gather all/any statements you have regarding retirement accounts from work or your family. Label this file "Retirement Accounts Information."

10. Gather any statements that you may have for investments (other than retirement accounts). You can call this file "Nonqualified Accounts Information," because they are investments you own outside your retirement account.

11. Round up all of your boring tax returns for the past seven years. Put them in a file labeled "Tax Returns Information."

If you don't have all of these documents, don't worry. The important thing is that you start now. One of the crucial steps to being budget lean and debt free is through tracking your most important information in these files. Besides, you may find a few extra bucks you never even knew you had. You may even be able to make a few new investments in the market for yourself!

Be sure to label your files and organize accordingly. When you are done, put the files in a safe and accessible place, like in a filing cabinet. Excellent work! You are now a great deal more organized than when you first picked up this book. You are also a step closer to seizing the day when it comes to your adventure on the money trail.

> "This is your life, your one and only life — so take excellence very personally."
> —**Scott Johnson**

Doing something positive for your life might require a sufficient amount of change, and change seldom comes easy. But the hardest part is over. You now know how important it is to hit the money trail. You know you are a capable adventurer, and you've organized one of the craziest parts of your life.

Completing this step alone is highly commendable, and you should be proud. You're one step further from becoming a statistic and one step closer to retiring worry free while creating the freedom to live your dreams.

> "To love oneself is the beginning of a
> lifelong romance."
> —**Oscar Wilde**

Switchback Terrain

Women face specific hurdles when it comes to their money that make it imperative to hit the money trail now! Women will most likely:

- outlive a partner by seven years or more.
- earn less than men (current estimate is $.72 on the dollar, or 28 percent less).
- accumulate less retirement benefits because on average women spend eleven years or more out of the workforce due to child rearing or care for elderly parents.

Note the three challenges you will face while hiking the money trail:

Challenge 1 Only 5 percent of Americans age sixty-five and over have annual incomes in excess of $25,000. Should you choose to marry and beat the divorce statistics of 50 percent for first marriages and 50 percent plus for second marriages, you should keep in mind that these numbers indicate that men have not done a great job historically of taking care of the family financial planning for retirement, i.e. you're hiking solo on the money trail!

Challenge 2 At current estimates, the Social Security Administration predicts that by the year 2013 the system will be paying out more than it is taking in, and unless Congress finds the money for a complete overhaul, there won't be enough in the fund to pay out full benefits. The current maximum anyone can receive from Social Security is $17,196 total per year, a whopping (not) $1,433 per month.

Challenge 3 On average, inflation is running at 4 percent per annum. That means your purchasing power will be cut nearly in half in fifteen years. The terrain you will be hiking on the money trail is going to cost you big-time, so make sure you're prepared!

Summit Checkpoints

Checkpoint 1 Bigger paychecks don't mean instant wealth. The more we make, the more we tend to spend. You work hard. Don't you deserve to keep some of what you make? Spend less than you make, and you will be pioneering a better hike on the money trail.

Checkpoint 2 You have all the equipment you need to get started with your money and investing right now. The latte factor can help you save $50 a month. That totals $600 a year, which invested annually in the market over forty years (with an assumed average market rate of return of at least 12 percent) could grow to more than $500,000 by the time you reach sixty-five. Remember, time is on your side, along with the wonderful power of compound interest!

chapter 2

Value-Packed
Goals

"You have to count on living every single day in a way you believe will make you feel good about your life."
—Jane Seymour

A s your guide on the money trail, I seek to outfit you with the tools you will need in order to have a fun, adventurous hike. In this chapter your task will be to properly identify your values tools and then equip yourself with them. By values tools, I'm referring to

what is most <u>meaningful</u> about money to you?

Your values could be something like having quality time, making a difference, freedom, or even happiness. Pioneering a fantastic financial plan for you begins with knowing your values and how they are directly linked to your goals. Personal financial planning means taking the time to really understand your values in relation to money.

Think of it this way: your money values will act as your compass. Once you align your values with money, you will absolutely *not* fall off the money trail. Your values—like a compass—will never steer you wrong when faced with challenges on and off the money trail. Be prepared to walk away from this chapter with a brand-new perspective.

This is not just a hike; it's a journey to new ways of thinking, believing, and behaving with your money. As your guide, I will always advise you to keep an open, upbeat mind while collecting your values tools.

"Make your own trail"
—Katharine Hepburn

TRAIL TALE...

In San Francisco I offer a two-hour financial seminar based on this book. Over the past couple of months the seminar has grown through word of mouth, and I've had the pleasure of meeting many interesting young women. When I reach Topic 2, where I discuss value-packed goals, the room always falls uncomfortably silent and I could swear I sense an unspoken moan.

I know that most of the young women who attend the financial seminar assume prior to their arrival that we will simply discuss the basics about money: retirement plans, the stock market, taxes. But it would be impossible to successfully hike the money trail without first equipping yourself with your values tools. After all, money means different things to different people. The sooner you realize what money specifically means to you, the easier it will be to apply that knowledge toward putting together an inspiring financial plan, which in turn will lead to getting what you want out of life.

Your values will be key tools that you will need to take with you on the money trail. The apex of it all is: what ideas about money ultimately feel good to you? There is no right or wrong here; there's just you and how you feel about money. Identifying your truth is one of your greatest tasks!

Other Young Women's Values Tools

To help get your creative juices flowing, take a look at what other women who have attended my homegrown financial seminar have had to say about values tools. Please keep in mind that each person, including you, will have different values tools.

Elizabeth said,

"I just want to feel like I have more time for everything. Plus, I want to be able to make up my schedule as the days go along, not to have to report to anybody!"

= **Money Value:** Time and Flexibility

Amy said,

"I want to know that if I got canned from my job tomorrow I wouldn't have to freak out over it!"

= **Money Value:** Security

Samantha said,

"I want to know that I can do what I want to do without my boyfriend or family telling me I can't. Yeah, to do what I want to do when I want to do it!"

= **Money Value:** Freedom

Alexa said,

"I want to give back. I want my life to have an impact on helping make things better in some way, to somehow help others!"

= **Money Value:** Helping Others

Julie said,

"I have a deep urge to explore, just to be able to go and see as much of this world as possible, to meet as many different types of people from different cultures as possible!"

= **Money Value:** Freedom to Travel

Christina said,

"I know that I should be doing something when it comes to my financial planning. I read the horrible statistics on women a couple of years ago and always feel really guilty when I think about not having gotten started with my own financial planning. It makes me feel scared that I will end up like a bag lady. Having a solid financial plan would be really good for me."

= Money Value: Financial Security and Peace of Mind

Lisa said,

"I have always lacked self-confidence. Ever since I can remember, I just felt really timid and shy. I want to take more pride in myself and my life's choices."

= Money Value: Confidence

Kathy said,

"I rush and rush all day long. I seem to be always on overload just trying to survive and manage my level of stress."

= Money Value: Calmness and Happiness

Sue said,

"I have always lacked motivation. Even in grade school I was a really talented swimmer, but I chose to quit the swim team just because it seemed like too much effort. I know I could do better. I just want to know what it would be like to reach my maximum potential!"

= Money Value: Realizing True Potential (Self-Actualizing)

Here is a full list of the values mentioned:

Calmness

Confidence

Financial Security

Flexibility

Freedom

Freedom to Travel

Happiness

Helping Others

Peace of Mind

Realizing True Potential (Self-Actualizing)

Security

Time

Do you notice that everything on this list has one important thing in common? Everything is an *idea* about what money can provide. These ideas, or values, are the most important things in your life. Why? Because you would do just about anything to achieve them. Simply put, they are who you genuinely are. No matter what is happening or not happening in your life, your values remain a constant.

The values you will need to identify are all pretty straightforward and simple. Sometimes it just takes a little exploring to come to some wonderful realizations of your true values. The reality is that most of us already know who we are and what is most important to us. Consider taking a little quiet time to reflect on your true money values. What types of ideas about money make you "buzz" with excitement?

Values Dysfunction

Let's say that what is important to you about money is time and flexibility, but your current job is a rigorous set schedule of fourteen-hour days that entails working a seventy-hour week— a clear indication that something is wrong, right? Your money values are out of line with your work schedule. Want another example? What if financial security is important to you, but instead of investing you've been using most of your paycheck to buy clothes and eat out? Again, your behavior with money is incompatible with your values.

You need to figure out if the way you currently live your life is compatible with your personal money values. If your values are incompatible with the choices you are making, it will be impossible to live a happy, fun, fulfilling life.

TRAIL TALE...

Usually, we subconsciously practice the money values we learned from our families as we were growing up. As I mentioned earlier, I grew up in Miami, Florida, with my mother, stepfather, and older sister. We lived a somewhat extravagant upper-middle-class eighties lifestyle. I was a lucky girl, at least in some respects!

Money was almost never discussed, except when my mother complained that my stepfather kept spending the money he earned as a banker before he was even able to make it. (Ring a bell? Remember "spending more than you make?") We had a ski house in Vermont, a beach house in the Florida Keys, and a family-style ranch house in Miami. As far back as I remember, our driveway always sported the latest BMWs, and my family had more than five country club memberships at the same time!

The strong but unspoken messages I received about money values were 1) spend more than you make, and 2) go out and get more stuff if you want to be happy. Consumption was supposed to lead to gratification and what we are all ultimately looking for, happiness.

From age seventeen to twenty-seven, I had three careers. In each career I subconsciously incorporated the family values I grew up with into my own lifestyle, and boy, oh boy, was I good at integrating those values. I consistently spent more than I made. My materialistic lifestyle never led me to happiness, just to more confusion, emptiness, and unhappiness.

Why Unhappiness?

The main source of angst in my life stemmed from the fact that I had not matched my money values with my personal values.

In 1998, by chance I came across a chapter in a book that led me to think about the concept of money values. Upon reflection I came to realize that my strongest and truest money values were time and flexibility, yet my lifestyle had nothing to do with those values. In other words, the life I had created for myself on the outside didn't reflect the person I really was inside. I continuously chose difficult, stressful, time-intensive jobs that offered high pay with little time or flexibility. Imagine. I spent ten years in several professional careers making money so I could go out and spend just as I saw my family do as I was growing up. Ever since I took the time to identify my money values, I have felt liberated from the subconscious pain of feeling out of sync with myself and how I live.

Break Your Family Cycle

Most people seem to unconsciously adopt their attitudes and behaviors about money early on, usually via their childhood experiences. By taking the time to sit down and identify your money values and then set personal goals based on them, you put yourself on "automatic ascension," meaning it will be a heck of a lot easier to reach your dreams!

> "There are some decisions in life that only you can make."
> —**Merie Shain**

Molly's Values Equipment

Molly, a good friend I met while living in Hong Kong, is a successful banker who has lived abroad for more than ten years. She has enjoyed traveling to beautiful locations, fine wines, beautiful clothes, an apartment filled with antiques, and gorgeous jewelry, some of life's finer material things.

This past summer Molly expressed to me a frustration with her expatriate lifestyle. On one of her visits to San Francisco, we sat in my office talking about her concerns and reviewing her monthly budget.

As I booted up my computer, I asked Molly what was most meaningful to her about money. She sat quietly for a moment in deep thought. She answered "security." I then asked her to define what security means to her.

Molly thought for a few moments more before responding, "To have the peace of mind that I can do what I want when I want." I then asked her, "What does doing what you want when you want entail?" She replied, "I suppose it means having the ability to leave Hong Kong and possibly move back to the States. Flexibility to change!"

There was a deep, long pause. I then said, "Now, Molly, let's pretend that you have security, peace of mind, and flexibility to make changes. What would then be important to you about being in that place?"

"I think I would feel freer and more fulfilled with the life I could create for myself. Plus, living stateside would offer me a greater sense of choices with men and the ability to create a long-term partnership in a place I would like to be for a long period of time."

As you can see, Molly started with *security* and *peace of mind*, which led to *flexibility*. For Molly, flexibility meant having the choice to move. Once Molly had this choice, she tapped into what was also important to her, *freedom* and *fulfillment*. With freedom and fulfillment she would have more choices to build a *long-term partnership*. Molly was thrilled to have uncovered and tapped into her true values!

Molly's Values List

1. Long-term partnership with a man—intimacy

2. More choices and options

3. Freedom and fulfillment

4. Flexibility in life choices—ability to change

5. Peace of mind

6. Security

Does Molly's values list match her current behavior with money?

As an investment banker abroad, Molly earned close to $150,000 a year, a considerable amount for any individual. Yet she had absolutely no savings and lived from paycheck to paycheck. One of the main reasons Molly felt pressured to stay in Hong Kong was to continue receiving her high expatriate compensation package.

We looked at Molly's monthly expenses to see where her money was going. This is what we saw:

Monthly Expense	Dollar Amount
Rent	$3,000
Parking	$500
Housekeeper	$300
Dry cleaning	$350
Clothes	$750
Eating out	$600
Cell phone	$150
Miscellaneous shopping	$500
Pleasure travel	$500
Total nonessentials*	$3,150
*(nonessential items = optional expenses)	

Shockingly, Molly was spending almost half of her take-home pay after taxes on nonessential items (in yellow type) costing more than $3,000! I gently pointed out to her that she was spending over $3,000 on things that had little or nothing to do with her values list. Why was this a problem for Molly? Because spending such a large amount of money on nonessentials each month didn't offer her the ability to tap into her true values. Once Molly could see that how she chose to spend her money was not in line with her values, she decided to cut back on her nonessential expenses. The only such expenses she decided to keep were her dry cleaning and housekeeper, since she felt that both offered her more freedom and flexibility, a part of her values list. Molly's new monthly budget looked like this:

Monthly Expense	Dollar Amount
Rent	$3,000
Parking	$500
Housekeeper	$300
Dry cleaning	$350
Clothes	$250
Eating out	$300
Cell phone	$50
Miscellaneous shopping	$200
Pleasure travel	$250
Total nonessentials*	$1,700

*(nonessential items = optional expenses)

Molly was able to cut back $1,440 per month on nonessential expenses that had little or nothing to do with her values. She could now use this money to begin creating her adventure backpacks, which we will talk about further in Chapter 3. Once Molly learned how to equip herself with her values tools and how to align them with her money, she was able to easily address cutting back on her spending patterns.

> "Besides the noble art of getting things done, there is the noble art of leaving things undone. The wisdom of life consists in the elimination of nonessentials."
>
> —Liu Yutang

Is how you currently choose to spend your money compatible with your values?

This question goes back to the folders you organized in Chapter 1. Those folders are a good source of information to see if, over the course of several months, your expenditures match your values. (Later in this chapter I will show you how to identify and list your values tools.) These folders will always provide a reality check, a true glimpse of whether your spending reflects your values.

As it turned out, Molly called me two months after we sat down at my office desk to say, "I have so much more clarity and sense of purpose in my life! I really understand now the importance of making sure that when I spend my money, doing so aligns with my values. For one of the first times I feel on track and really in control of my life. A great sense of fulfillment and possibility has overcome me in the last couple of months."

In the same conversation Molly mentioned that since taking the time to equip herself with her values. tools and review her monthly expenses, she had found new ways to cut back without sacrificing the "quality" in her life. She found a fully furnished service apartment at half the price of her current apartment in Hong Kong, and she could pay rent for it on a month-to-month basis. Molly decided that she would then ship her furniture to the States to be stored. That way if a great job opportunity arose there, it would be easier for her to pick up and move. Best of all, her monthly savings now amounted to a whopping grand total of $3,940! Molly went on to thank me, and all I could do was gush with great joy for the excitement I heard in my friend's voice from way over there in Asia!

> "Friends are kind to each other's hopes. They cherish each other's dreams."
> —Henry David Thoreau

I know that most of us would love to be able to save some $4,000 a month, and I do realize that compensation packages for expatriates working abroad tend to be inflated by more than 50 percent of what you would receive if you worked in your own country. Please do not let the size of the numbers in Molly's story throw you off. What is most important about her situation is that she was able to take a closer look at herself and what was truly important to her when she examined her values tools. In doing so, she was able to stop wasting her time, energy, and resources in ways that didn't fit her on a core level. She was able to tap into the flow of her life—and her money—by clarifying who she was and in what direction she wanted to go.

What is most meaningful
to you about money?

"Decision is a risk rooted in the
courage of being free."
—Paul Tillich

I think by now you can appreciate the different types of choices you make when it comes to your money. Those choices will directly affect your friendships, the type of relationship you choose to be in, what you think you deserve, what you get, and how you live, to name but a few. And let's not forget the overall quality of your life.

Money affects each and every one of us differently according to what we hold as important. Don't you think it's worthwhile to take the time to sit and ponder what is most meaningful about money to you? Why do you make the choices you make when it comes to your money?

Now it's your turn
to take a look at your
values tools.

Let's find out what your values are about money. In the following exercise, I want you to keep asking yourself, "What is the most meaningful thing about money to me?" When you come up with one value, ask yourself, "What is meaningful to me about (*fill in with your value*)?" And keep going from there. To give you a head start, take a look at the following sample list of values.

Sample Values List

Intimacy	Having more time
Independence	Being more loving
Being calmer	Flexible schedule
Enjoyment	Greater spirituality
Freedom	Confidence
Security	Connection with others
Happiness	Fulfillment
Peace of mind	Knowledge
Power	Being the best
Helping others	Making a difference
Helping family	Fun
Realizing my true potential (self-actualization)	Growing
	Adventure
Pride	Inner peace
Self-worth	Balance
Achievement	Providing for family

Now it's your turn to try. Start at number six and work your way up to number one. After each value you list, continue to ask yourself what is most meaningful to you about money. Ready, set, take a deep breath, try to relax, and go for it!

Your Values List

#1 _____

#2 _____

#3 _____

#4 _____

#5 _____

#6 _____

Now, that wasn't too difficult, was it? Take a moment to read and reread the values you have listed. This is who you are, and remember that you can do anything when you make choices that reflect who you are at the core. If you take care to align your money choices with your values, you are building a strong platform base to work off of when it comes down to the overall direction of your life. Excited? And so you should be. You are truly embarking on an awesome adventure, one that will absolutely enhance your life.

> "By being yourself, you put something
> wonderful in the world
> that was not there before."
> —Edwin Elliot

Goal Gathering

Now that you have equipped yourself with your values tools, it's time to map out your goals. Why? Because setting goals allows you to determine and achieve what you want out of your financial life. Remember earlier when you identified your money values? Well, now you can use those values to help you express your goals, which in turn will help you put your values into practice.

> "A great goal in life is
> the only fortune worth finding."
> —Jacqueline Kennedy Onassis

TRAIL NOTES FOR GREAT GOAL SETTING

TRAIL NOTE 1: Write your goals down.

Goals absolutely must be written down, no ifs, ands, or buts on this one! Writing your goals down is probably one of the most important things you can ever do. You cannot talk about a wish list and hope it will happen, but this is what most people do.

Please do not be one of them. When you sit to ponder your goals, you will be opening a door to your very own "Fantasy Island." But to ensure that you actually get the opportunity to visit the island, you must write your goals down. The amount of power in this one simple act is just amazing.

TRAIL TALE...

When I moved back to San Francisco a year ago, I sat down to review and rewrite some of my goals. One of my short-term goals was to help motivate and educate other women my age to start investing their money. At the time I had no idea how I would accomplish this goal. After all, Wall Street opportunities that focused on educational programs for this demographic were nil. How would I get a job involved in this field?

As the weeks passed I began to think more about how I had learned the basics about money and investing. I had attended nonprofit conferences with book authors who had written motivational materials to help women baby boomers start investing their money. As I thought about the market, it became evident to me that I wanted to write a motivational book on money and investing for my generation of women. As I continued to think through the idea of writing a book, I had another interesting idea. Why not create a nonprofit foundation that would seek to motivate, inspire, and educate women my age about their money, investing, and the vital importance of saving for retirement? There was obviously a gap in the market when it came to financial educational information for young women.

Simply through the power of writing down my short-term goals, my mind, both consciously and subconsciously, was able to go straight to work figuring out how to make this goal a reality. Once I had realized how to do that, I quickly began planning what I needed to do financially to make this a reality. And yes, I also double-checked to make sure this goal was in line with my values. You see, once I wrote my goal down, it became very real and very powerful. I'm sure that my mind was working overtime, even in my sleep, to try to figure out how to make this short-term goal a reality.

Your goals will never amount to anything unless you write them down! This is an incredible technique; do not let it pass you by!

"Set your goals to paper
and you are halfway there."
—Don Ward

TRAIL NOTE 2:
Review your goals.

You will need to take a monthly time-out to review your goals. At our age, things change often, as do our emotions and what we want out of life. That's because we are experiencing so many new things for the first time. When you take the time to review the goals you've set for yourself, you are giving your mind a "refresher," which will help you continue to make these goals a reality. You will reaffirm your focus in life both in your mind and to yourself.

TRAIL NOTE 3:
Share your goals.

Some people believe their goals should be kept secret, just like their journals. The truth is that when you share your goals with others, you are allowing the whole world to try to help you accomplish them. That means other people can really get behind you. You're allowing others to offer you whatever assistance and support they can to help you achieve your goals.

> "Surround yourself with people who believe you can."
> —**Dan Zadra**

When I decided to write this book, I began chatting about the idea with all my friends. And yes, a couple of them looked at me like I was crazy, which kind of made me wonder if they were my friends at all or if they were just pretending to be. Shortly thereafter I took a road trip to Los Angeles to visit my oldest and dearest friend, L.J., someone I met when I moved to New York City at the age of seventeen.

It had been quite a while since L.J. and I had caught up with each other, and the occasion was joyous when I got to his house. After I settled in, L.J. asked, "So what are you up to these days, V?" I answered, "I'm thinking about writing a book for young women like myself on money and investing, you know, to help motivate them to get started." I will never forget his encouragement. "Vanessa, that is just awesome. I know you could do anything you set your mind to. I know the book will be a great success." When you're dancing around in the land of ideas and "I think I cans" alone, this kind of positive feedback from a close friend is exactly what you need to hear!

> "It's seizing the day and accepting responsibility for your future. It's seeing what other people don't see, and pursuing that wisdom no matter who tells you not to."
> —**Howard Schultz**

TRAIL NOTE 4:
Make sure your values are compatible with your goals.

Earlier in this chapter we discussed the importance of equipping yourself with your values tools, and you went through the process of identifying them. You can now use those values to help you set goals. For example, let's say that on your values list you had confidence. You could set a short-term goal for yourself to get a promotion and a raise at your current job within three to six months, which would in turn help you achieve confidence through your professional career. Remember: develop goals that help you put your values into practice.

TRAIL NOTE 5:
Make your goals as detailed as possible.

Think about adding detail and depth to your goals. If you've written down something vague and intangible, how will you ever be able to prove that you've achieved it? And if you can't *prove* that you can achieve your goal, it isn't a goal, it's just a wish. For example, you shouldn't just write down, "I will be free of student loans." You need to write down details about how you will achieve this goal, like, "I will pay off my student loans in the next sixteen months by taking a roommate, which will allow me to put the extra $600 I save in rent toward paying off my student loans. I will also take a part-time job on the weekends at my aunt's antique store, which will help me pay off another $200 of my student loans per month. Instead of paying off my student loans in thirty-six months, I will pay them off now in sixteen months."

A Tenacious Task

A useful checkpoint in setting goals is to ask yourself, "Where do I want to be in one year?" One year is a key period of time to begin imagining where you would like to be and what you would like to happen in your life in the meantime. In fact, you could easily change your entire life in that period of time. Now is the time for you to stop, examine your thoughts, and write down what you specifically want out of your life. This list is all about you and for you. You can always go back and alter it, but you are not allowed to skip this step. Everyone has to start somewhere. Once you identify a few of your goals, other goals will begin to appear. To make this a little easier, I'm going to offer you a sample goal list to fill out. Remember, this is all about getting started today!

> "Your hopes, dreams, and aspirations are legitimate. They are trying to take you airborne, above the clouds, above the storms— if you will only let them!"
> —**Diane Roger**

Sample Short-Term Goals

Take up a new hobby
Lose weight
Start contributing monthly to my 401(k)
Go to college
Travel
Redecorate
Start a business

Sample Mid-Term Goals

Get a new job that pays more money
Leave my boyfriend
Buy more designer shoes
Start a retirement plan
Take a year off to live in another country
Get a new car

Sample Long-Term Goals

Quit smoking/drinking
Pay off student loans
Pay off credit card debt
Buy a house
Have a million bucks
Make new friends

OTHER TRAIL NOTES

On the following page, fill one to five goals for each stage of goals, short-term (three to six months), mid-term (one to two years), and long-term (two to five years).

For all of your goals remember to ask yourself:

Who will I share this goal with?

What values is this goal compatible with?

Have I added enough detail to make this a goal and not a wish?

Short-Term Goals (three to six months)

#1 _____

#2 _____

#3 _____

#4 _____

#5 _____

Mid-Term Goals (one to two years)

#1 _____

#2 _____

#3 _____

#4 _____

#5 _____

Long-Term Goals (two to five years)

#1 _____

#2 _____

#3 _____

#4 _____

#5 _____

Awesome Way to Be!

Feel accomplishment and pride for your efforts here! Please do not criticize yourself or feel badly if this is not an easy process. It might take a couple of times for you to sit quietly and think about your values and goals, both personal and professional, before you can feel comfortable with what you have come up with. The more you do this exercise, the easier it will become.

You are now taking responsibility for your future. By equipping yourself with your values tools and setting goals that are in line with them, you are opening yourself up to the unlimited possibilities of the journey of your life. Way to go! Time to climb to the next plateau.

Switchback Terrain

- Before hitting the money trail, you will need to equip yourself with your values tools. Pioneering a fantastic financial plan begins with identifying those values. Begin by asking yourself this question: "What is meaningful about money to me?" Remember, your values are a type of idea that you have about money, such as time, flexibility, and security.

- Make sure your behavior with money is compatible with your values. Determine if the way you currently live is compatible with your personal values when it comes to money.

- Once equipped with your values tools, you can use them to help you express your goals, which will in turn help you put your values into practice. Setting these types of goals will enable you to live your dreams as a carefree hiker on the money trail.
- Trail notes to great goal setting include
  1. writing your goals down
  2. reviewing your goals
  3. sharing your goals
  4. making sure that your values are compatible with your goals
  5. trying to add as much detail as possible

chapter 3

Gear Up: Budget Lean and Debt Free

"Years may wrinkle the skin,
but to give up enthusiasm
wrinkles the soul."
—Samuel Ullman

In Chapter 1 we left off with your getting organized, and in Chapter 2 we identified your values tools and began mapping out your short-term, mid-term, and long-term financial goals. Now it's time to figure out where you truly stand today on the money scale and shortcuts to making your money go the long distance. I will also help you take a closer look at hazardous money trail signs: credit card debt and student loans. In other words, do you track your debt, or does your debt track you?

Ready? Time to Climb!

Where do you think you stand financially?

For most of us, what we think we "weigh" and what we actually "weigh" on the money scale happen to be two very different numbers. Do you know what it costs for you to live each month? Do you budget federal, state, and local taxes into your monthly cost of living? Most of us believe or deceive ourselves into believing that we spend less than we actually do to keep up our current quality of life. We might even believe we are budget lean when we're not! Why? The way we choose to spend our money each month often doesn't include many miscellaneous expenses.

For Example:

- Do you belong to a gym? If so, is this a monthly expense or do you pay to renew each year?

- Do you pay your car insurance premium monthly or bimonthly?

- Did you go to a friend's wedding last year? Did you include this travel expense in your budget?

- If you pay your own electricity bill, do you include the additional cost per month of heating your apartment or house in winter? That could be an extra $40 per month for the three coldest months of the year!

- Do you have a pet? Do you take it to be groomed once in a while? How about a visit to the vet every six months?

- Do you get your hair cut and colored every six weeks? Did you factor in this cost?
- How about your magazine subscriptions?
- A bottle of expensive perfume from the department store counters here and there?
- How about a tune-up for your car? The odd oil change?
- Did you forget birthday, wedding, and holiday gifts for friends and family, plus housewarmings?
- Did you have an unexpected dental visit recently? Perhaps a teeth cleaning?

See how the little stuff adds up to much bigger stuff without even a blink? Remember the power of the latte factor that we discussed in Chapter 1? Well, the examples listed above are other reminders that small, infrequent expenses add up to make big differences on the money scale.

"Look the world straight in the eye."
—**Helen Keller**

I understand that it can be shocking to recognize how all of these little things add up to so much. But the flip side is that once you take the courageous step of identifying your true costs, you will be equipped with the truth, the truth of where you stand on your money scale. With the truth in hand, you will be able to plan appropriately and accurately, empowering yourself to a brighter and happier financial journey.

> "The great enemy of the truth is very often not the lie—deliberate, contrived, and dishonest—but the myth—persistent, persuasive, and unrealistic."
> —**John F. Kennedy**

Managing Your Money Supply

Time to get out your bank statements, ATM slips, credit card bills, and any other receipts for how you've spent your money in the last year. Begin to make categories for all of the different types of expenses you have incurred. I know this will take time to do, but just think about all of the hours you worked this week—forty, fifty, sixty? Don't you think you deserve just a couple of hours to shed some light on what your money scale looks like today, and then to plan where your financial journey will be going tomorrow?

Let's think about this for a second. You spend immeasurable amounts of time each week working for someone else to help make *their* business a success; don't you deserve to make sure *your* financial life is a success, too? This way you can hike the money trail of life physically fit, enjoying the scenery along the way. It's absolutely imperative that you make time for you in this very special way. I can promise you this: most of our mothers did not take the time to do this, because taking care of money matters "wasn't the norm." I firmly believe that my mother would have had the life she believed she deserved and subconsciously wanted if she had taken the time to do this.

This is about making positive choices for yourself. And believe you me, I know we all have many choices to make in this lifetime! How about making choices that will help create the opportunities and a platform for you to build a happy, fulfilling financial life? By choosing to respect yourself and to gear up budget lean you are creating those very opportunities for the amazingly wonderful and creative you.

So, Let's Get Cracking!

On a sheet of paper, make expense categories—auto insurance, telephone, cell phone, electricity, rent, miscellaneous gifts, travel, hair care, etcetera—for each month. Next, add the amount you spent in each category each month over the past year. Once you've done this, total how much you spent in the past year for each category. Now divide each category total by twelve. This will tell you how much you spent on average each month last year on each category. Now add each category together to equal your total expenses per month. This number is what it costs you to live each month. Take that number now and multiply it by twelve. This is what it truly costs you to live each year (please keep in mind that this doesn't take taxes into consideration). You could call this number the bare bones of what you need to live on.

"It is our responsibilities, not ourselves, that we should take seriously."
—Peter Ustinov

I suggest that you keep a monthly budget that will offer details of how you spend your money. If you work off a Microsoft Windows application on your computer, you can easily create a folder called "Budget" that will hold twelve Microsoft Excel files named after each month of the year. (You can also easily create this budget on notebook paper.) Make a template for yourself by listing all of your different expense categories in the left column; you can then add actual dollar amounts for each item in the right column. As you can see from the Sample Budget listed on the facing page, a few categories may be left blank. Remember, there will be expenses that you do not incur on a monthly basis. But it will be easier for you not to miss an infrequent expense if you list the category each month.

I find working with the Excel program quick, easy, and readily adaptable for making changes to account for unexpected expenses any time. The idea is to keep up with these files frequently. It really only takes a few seconds to review your monthly budget. Knowing the reality of where you stand financially today will help you become more respectful of your money and how you choose to spend it tomorrow.

EXAMPLE: AVERAGE MONTHLY EXPENSES	
Vanessa's Sample Budget June 2001	
Health insurance	$91.00
Hair trim	$130.00
Cell phone	$58.00
Rent	$1,438.00
Auto insurance	$750.00
Auto lease	$274.00
Telephone	$62.93
DSL connection fee	$36.42
Electricity	$21.42
Monthly cash allowance	$1,400.00
Advisor license fees	$62.50
Domain host fee	$39.90
Cable	$10.00
Travel	
Car maintenance	
Dental	
Yoga fee	$50.00
Miscellaneous	
TOTAL	$3,749.17

How to Hike "This Way" and Budget "That Way"

If you started this exercise knowing exactly where you weigh in on the money scale, chances are that you have reconfirmed what you already knew. For those of you who did not weigh in budget lean, you have confirmed that you spend more than you thought.

Make sure you know what your net income is after taxes!

Pull out your last paycheck and take a close look at it. You will see the gross income amount somewhere at the top. Now, after your federal, state, local, Social Security, and Medicare taxes, what are you left with? This is what is called your net income.

Your gross income (before taxes) is _____

and your net income (after taxes) is_____

TRAIL NOTES on Cutting Back on Your Spending Money

Cutting back on your spending money isn't about taking drastic measures or depriving yourself. Cutting back is about shaving off a little here and a little there as you see fit so that the numbers add up and you don't sacrifice your quality of life. Some of your monthly expense categories—rent, car insurance, etcetera—will be fixed amounts. Other categories will fluctuate depending on how much you decide to spend each year. How about your haircut or coloring? Can you do this every eight weeks instead of six, hence saving a whole two months' worth of haircut and/or coloring expenses a year? How about when you travel; do you buy the $5 headphones to watch the in-flight movie? Why not bring your own headphones? If you travel ten times in one year, that's a savings of $50! Can you do your own nails? How about your magazine subscriptions; can you do without one? Do you currently have the most competitive cell phone plan? If so, can you cut back on the number of minutes you use each month, perhaps shaving another twenty-five bucks off your monthly budget? You see, with each decision you make on how to spend each dollar, you are gaining a sense of control and power over your money.

This type of plan is what I like to call a nonlimiting budget, kind of like the diet you go on where the instructions allow you to eat whatever you want, whenever you want, until you are full! You are not limiting what you can spend each month, so you don't feel deprived. More important, you're deciding how to spend your budgeted money each month. You're making choices for yourself that allow you to be conscious of how you spend your money and can then enjoy doing so without the guilt.

Hiking the money trail is not just about having money; it's about having power over that money.

MORE TRAIL NOTES to Keep You in Check with Your Money Supply

Never, ever spend more than $100 without giving yourself twenty-four hours to think about it!

How many times have you sauntered into a clothing store that had the hippest, latest merchandise practically jumping off the hangers at you? The music was pumping and the sales staff hopped around to the beat, offering you knowing glances that said, "So what are you waiting for? Time to spend, spend, spend!" You are completely lured into an impulse purchase of a $200 cashmere sweater...a sweater you don't really need. Then, later in the day or even the next day, you feel tremendous guilt for racking up another two hundred bucks on your credit card, and it hits you (drum roll, please)—buyer's remorse! By using the twenty-four-hour method, you will offer yourself the opportunity to think it over and decide clearly, without outside distractions, if you really want to spend X amount of money on X item.

Know what you spend!

Write down all of your ATM or bank withdrawals and purchases from your money market account (we will discuss the advantages of this type of account in Chapter 4) or checking account each and every time you use your ATM or bank card. Again, this type of behavior allows you to know exactly where you stand and gives you that good old sense of power over your money that I keep mentioning. If you are in a store or at the ATM, whip out a pen and write down in your checkbook register what you've spent or withdrawn. This method will help you see where you spend money recklessly and where it makes sense for you to cut back.

Another helpful hint is to go to the ATM once a week. It's easier to keep track of how much you withdraw, stay within your cash budget allowance, and write it down if withdrawing money is a weekly instead of a sporadic event. In my monthly budget I make a weekly cash allowance for myself. Each Monday I hit the ATM and withdraw my $350. If there's a little something extra I need to pick up later in the week that I haven't budgeted for, I try to spend less of that week's cash allowance to save for that extra expense. Again, you will be making choices on how to spend your money.

Pay with cash!

By spending with cash instead of a credit card, you will automatically force yourself to think much harder about how you spend your money. Many have favored the cash-only system when it comes to addressing spending habits. Try it out for yourself; I promise that it won't let you down!

Nix a few credit cards!

Get rid of a few credit cards. None is best. If you just have to have a credit card, make sure it's only one, not three like the average American. I will talk at length about credit cards vs. ATM debit cards later in this chapter.

Congratulations!

You now know how to empower yourself through getting down to the nitty-gritty honesty of how you spend your money. Now you can see exactly where you stand on the money scale and can gear up to be budget lean.

> "This time, like all times, is a very good one, if we but know what to do with it."
> —**Ralph Waldo Emerson**

Credit Card Debt and You

Have you been suckered into how great your credit card company or companies think you are? Did they keep offering you higher and higher "available" limits on your card, making you think that you really deserved to be spending more? Did they offer you blank checks you could use to get cash off your credit card? I bet they might even have been nice enough to offer to let you skip a payment, just to show you how great they think you are!

Well, so very sorry to break the bad news to you, girl. You, like most of us, have been seduced by the credit card companies. They've sought you out. After all, with the current average annual percentage rate at 17.9 percent, their profit margins are huge!

Say you are thirty and have racked up five thousand bucks' worth of credit card debt. If your annual percentage interest rate was 18 percent on the card and you made minimal monthly payments, how long would it take you to pay off the $5,000? Guess again? Forty-six fricken long years! Even more shocking is the fact that you would have also paid $18,941 whopping smackaroos in interest.

If you are a victim of credit card debt, you are so not alone. How do you know if you're a victim? If you can't pay off your credit card debts today, then you are a victim of the savvy media play on how superb credit cards are. But credit card debt is no laughing matter. It is quite serious, as it could keep you from building a happy, solid financial future.

Here's the Scoop

If you have more than one credit card, gather up your statements. Take a look at all of your outstanding balances and begin to make a list, like the sample list below, of these balances. Add to the list the annual percentage rate you are currently offered on each card.

Sample List		
Creditor	Balance Owed	Interest Rate
Clothing Store	$1,500	20%
Master Card	$1,750	15%
Dad	$500	0%
Visa	$1,500	8.9%

Way to be! Congratulate yourself for exposing the truth about you and your credit card debt. Feel like you're bonding with your debt? Good, let's keep going!

Compacting Your Credit Card Debt

Time to think of consolidating your debt by switching it all to one credit card, the card with the lowest annual percentage rate. If you do not have a credit card that is offering you a low annual percentage rate (low in today's market is something like 5.9 percent), then apply for one that offers you this rate. Keep in mind that credit card companies really want your business, and if you have a good credit history they should make it very easy for you to switch to a credit card they are offering.

Not sure if the interest rates you get on your credit card make that big a difference? Think again, sister. Take a look at the adjacent chart to see how taking a little extra time to shop around for a better interest rate can make a big difference in the long run. The chart assumes that you owe $4,000.

If you decide to shop around for a lower rate, check out the Web site *www.cardweb.com* (301-631-9100). It offers a ton of detailed information on different credit cards, rates, fees, and perks, such as frequent flyer awards.

Make sure you read *all* of the fine print on any information you receive from credit card companies. Remember earlier when we chatted about respect, respect for you and your money? Well, time to make time again. I know it would be much

EFFECT OF INTEREST RATES ON A DEBT OF $4,000

Annual %Rate	Monthly Payment	Debt paid off	Total Interest Paid
5.9%	$100	45 Months	$465
5.9%	$110	40 Months	$417
5.9%	$150	29 Months	$298
5.9%	$200	22 Months	$221
7.9%	$100	47 Months	$658
7.9%	$110	42 Months	$587
7.9%	$150	30 Months	$413
7.9%	$200	22 Months	$304
9.9%	$100	49 Months	$874
9.9%	$110	44 Months	$775
9.9%	$150	31 Months	$536
9.9%	$200	21 Months	$389
12.9%	$100	53 Months	$1,257
12.9%	$110	47 Months	$1,101
12.9%	$150	32 Months	$739
12.9%	$200	23 Months	$528
15.9%	$100	58 Months	$1,736
15.9%	$110	50 Months	$1,494
15.9%	$150	34 Months	$968
15.9%	$200	24 Months	$678
18.9%	$100	63 Months	$2,362
18.9%	$110	54 Months	$1,986
18.9%	$150	35 Months	$1,229
18.9%	$200	25 Months	$842

Source: *9 Steps to Financial Freedom* by Suze Orman (Crown Publishing Company, 1997)

more fun to see a movie or meet a girlfriend for lunch, but you need to know the facts about what you've signed up for. Once equipped with this information, you will be able to make good, solid decisions about your credit card debt that could ultimately save you hundreds of dollars a year. Remember, this has to do with keeping more of that hard-earned money that you make. Once you become aware of what you really owe and where you stand, you will free up energy to go and be the best possible empowered you, free of money worries!

In Your Best Interest

If you've been a pack rat and have some savings lying around, it could be a wise idea to use that savings to help pay off your credit card debt. Why? Because the interest rate that you could be paying on your credit card debt could be higher than what you could possibly hope to receive on any investments. If you pay off your credit card debt that has an 18 percent annual percentage rate, you are in effect choosing to pay yourself a tax-free rate of return of 18 percent.

Confused? Let me explain. Pretend you have a choice between paying off a $1,000 credit card bill at an 18 percent annual percentage rate and keeping $1,000 in a money market account with a 5 percent rate of return. If you don't pay off the loan (i.e., credit card debt) in a year, you will have racked up $180 in interest on your debt. As for your money market account, you will have made fifty bucks in interest. Hence, between paying interest on your debt and earning interest in your money market account, you are down $130 for the year. The better scenario would be to use the $1,000 to pay off your debt so you pay no interest — and also earn no interest. By doing this, you will save paying $130 in interest for the year!

TRAIL NOTES
on How Your Credit Cards Work

What's the difference between the average daily balance and the two-cycle average daily balance?

A grande difference! Note that the average daily balance is the calculating interest plan that you want from your credit card company. With the average daily balance, the issuer of your credit card will divide the year up into thirty-day billing cycles. On the last day of each billing cycle, the issuer calculates your bill and mails it to you. Say you owe $1,000. If you pay the entire amount on the due date, you won't pay any interest. But if you leave even $1 unpaid, you get hit with interest charges on your next bill based on the average daily balance of your billing cycle. In this example, your balance would be $1,000 for twenty-five days of the billing cycle, and $1 for the last five days, resulting in an average daily balance of $833 on which you will be required to pay interest!

I know that doesn't sound like a very fair scenario. Well, with the two-cycle average daily balance method, it's even worse. Your credit card company calculates the amount of interest you owe based on the average daily balance over the last two billing cycle periods, in effect making the amount on which interest is calculated even greater.

The difference between using a credit card that calculates interest based on the average daily balance as opposed to the two-month average daily balance could be the difference between paying more than 50 percent plus in interest payments, particularly if your habit has been to charge and then pay the balance off two months later. Be smart and make sure you are signed up for the average daily balance method.

Should I pay an annual fee for my credit card?

Nope. As I mentioned earlier, credit card companies are competing for your business. Paying an annual fee when hundreds of credit card companies are vying for your business is something you don't need to do. In fact, if you find one credit card company you like that offers a competitive annual percentage rate but charges a fee, give them a call. Explain nicely that you are a potential customer and would be happy to give them your business if they waived the annual fee for good. I betcha they will!

Do I want a high minimum monthly balance or a low one?

The answer is high. Credit card companies benefit from you having a low minimum monthly balance because it will take you longer to pay off your credit card balance. Hence, they make more money. Remember, the more you owe the longer it will take you to pay it off. Go with a higher rate on this one!

Should I use my cash advance privileges?

Absolutely not! Even if you may have a low introductory rate, say 5.9 percent, issuers will still charge you a percentage fee of the cash advance, say 2.5 percent. They may also charge you a huge interest rate on your cash advance. This is how many issuers get a huge bang for their buck.

Should I use a secured credit card?

Possibly. This type of credit card requires you to provide collateral by depositing money into a special savings account. Why? It was set up for customers who have defaulted on a loan in recent years and have had a difficult time finding an issuer who will take the chance on giving them a credit card. Although I don't like the idea of the issuer of a secured card taking your money and letting it sit in a no- or low-rate savings account while you use the card, this option could be a good near-term solution to help you build your credit and to show that you can be responsible and trusted.

What is a grace period?

Most credit card companies offer you grace periods that begin the day your purchases are made or posted (officially recorded) and last until the due date specified on the bill. If you pay your bill in full before the due date, you will not be charged any interest. If you carry a balance month to month, even a very small one, you lose the grace period.

How will credit card companies make money if I don't carry a balance?

Credit card companies make money in three ways:

- from the interest you pay
- from annual fees
- from the fee the credit card companies charge merchants

Recently, some credit card issuers have snuck in an extra fee of approximately $25 they charge customers who do not incur any interest charges over the course of the year. Imagine that, penalizing you for being good!

There are other good questions you want to be sure to ask when applying for a new card or finding out more information on your existing cards. Like, what is the annual percentage rate?

How long will the rate last? Some credit card companies will offer you teaser rates. A teaser rate is a low rate that applies for a year or less. After that time period, the rate usually increases dramatically. If you think you can pay off your debt within that time period, that card may be right for you in the short term. Again, make sure that you read all of the fine print; some rates apply only to transferred balances and not to new purchases.

Tracking Your Debt Before It Tracks You

I know that we young gals need to establish our credit for future home purchases, auto loans, small business loans, etcetera. But we don't need five credit cards to do this. We need only one. And if you already have good credit, you really don't need any! I understand that most people feel very uncomfortable "being" without a credit card. If you are one of them, make sure you get the best deal possible on yours and pay the bill as soon as it arrives.

Adventure on your money trail with ATM Debit Cards

One of the best ways to charge these days is with an ATM debit card. ATM debit cards can easily be acquired through opening a money market account (again, we will discuss money market accounts in detail in Chapter 4) that will offer you a competitive interest rate, free checking, ATM usage, and no annual fee.

What is also great about these cards is that you can easily track what you spend. All of your expenses—miscellaneous charges, ATM cash withdrawals, and paying bills—are consolidated into this one account. As discussed earlier in the Trail Notes on how to cut back on spending money, you should always record each of these expenses in your checkbook. It's super easy to track your expenditures, particularly with your ATM debit card acting as a credit card, too. Plus, no need to worry if you remembered to pay your credit card bill on time.

Take a glance at my ATM debit card checkbook expenditures for the week of January 1.

EXPENDITURES, ONE WEEK

Number/ Date	Description of Transaction	Payment/ Debit	Deposit/ Credit	Balance
1/01	Cash/ATM	$100		
1/01	Pharmacy	$30		
1/03	Mexican dinner	$25		
1/03	Nails	$20		
1/03	Grocery store	$30		
1/05	Office supplies	$40		
1/07	Chinese dinner	$25		
	Total cash for first week =	$270		

As you can see, I used $270 in cash for the first week in January. As I mentioned earlier, my current cash allowance is $350 per week. At the end of week one in January, I have an extra eighty bucks of my cash allowance. I now have the choice, guilt free, to spend it, invest it in a mutual fund, or just keep it for an unexpected expense later in the month. Either way, I will know that I am living within my means (which is huge!) and that I have guilt-free options with this extra $80.

It's okay to "get by with a little help from..."

If you're someone who's not willing to cut back to one card right now, or your debt feels way too overwhelming to even begin to know where to start, there is help! A nonprofit organization called Myvesta has been set up to help talk with you about your debt and how to address it. Myvesta offers you a free consultation to see which of their many different types of plans would be right for you. Unlike other debt consolidators, Myvesta also offers you a money coach and counseling if needed to help identify your issues with money, meaning whether being a shopaholic or spendaholic is a symptom of an underlying problem that needs to be addressed. Myvesta can help you identify the problem. Remember, there is absolutely no shame in consciously choosing to seek guidance and learning to live a happier, healthier life. Their Web site is packed with great information. Take a look at *www.myvesta.org* (800-680-3328).

Remember, you are not alone when it comes to credit card debt, and you have absolutely nothing to be ashamed about. This isn't the time to blame and criticize yourself for racking up debt. This is the time to roll up your sleeves and get busy finding out as much information as possible about how to make a plan to "off" your credit card debt once and for all!

> "Your proper concern is alone
> the action of your duty, not the fruits
> of the action. Cast them away,
> all desire and fear for the fruits,
> and perform your duty."
> —**The Bhagavad Gita**

TRAIL NOTES
on Student Loans

If you have outstanding student loans, here is the Trail Notes version of options available to you on paying them back or just lowering your monthly interest payments. If you're in a financial bind, you may even qualify to defer payment; so listen up. And please keep in mind, girls—these loans *must* be paid back. Defaulting on your student loan, as on any other type of loan, is serious business!

If you default on your loan, your school, the lender or agency that holds your loan, the state, and the federal government may all take action to recover the money, including notifying national credit bureaus of your default. This could affect your credit rating for a long time. For example, you may find it very difficult to borrow from a bank to buy a car or a house.

In addition, if you default, the agency holding your loan may ask your employer to deduct payments from your paycheck. Also, you may be liable for expenses incurred in collecting the loan. If you decide to return to school, you're not entitled to receive any more federal student aid. The U.S. Department of Education may even ask the Internal Revenue Service to withhold your income tax refund and apply it toward the amount you owe.

Now that we've gotten that little nugget of information out of the way, on to a few strategies to keep in mind when it comes to your student loans.

Know what you owe!

It's important to keep good records of what you owe and to whom you owe it. If you aren't certain how many student loans you obtained, contact the financial aid office of each school you attended and request a list of any loans received and the name of the lender from whom you obtained each loan. This information will not only help you track your obligations, it's required if you decide to:

Consolidate your loans. Loan consolidation pays off your existing student loans and reestablishes the balance in a single loan with one monthly payment. Loan consolidation offers you the flexibility to extend your repayment term and lower your monthly payment. Keep in mind that while you will make lower monthly payments, you will also pay more interest over the life of the loan. Be sure to try to attain a lower rate of interest on your loan if you choose to go down the consolidation path.

Refinance your loans. Whether you have one or more student loans, refinancing is always a good option to review. As interest rates constantly fluctuate with changes in the economy, locking in the current balance of your loan at an interest rate more than 1 percent below where it is now could mean a good chunk of savings each month on what you pay.

Prepay your loans. If you are not saddled by other high-rate debt, consider repaying your student loans first. One easy way to do this is by doubling your payment each month. Let's say you owe $10,000 on your student loans with an interest rate of 7.43 percent. If you assume interest rates will remain constant and that you will pay back your loan over ten years, your monthly payment will be $118. If you choose to double that amount and pay $236 a month, you will pay off your loan in four years and two months while saving more than $2,500 in interest. Keep in mind that prepayment of your student loans only makes sense if the interest rates on your loans are higher than the rates you can earn on an investment.

> > > > **more TRAIL NOTES!**

Uncle Sammy and Sallie Mae

The U.S. Department of Education, which administers the federal program run by Uncle Sammy, should be your first stop in finding out more information about your loans and if you are eligible for consolidation and one of several repayment options. The second stop should be Sallie Mae (the Student Loan Marketing Association), a company that services about a third of all student loans and is competitive with Uncle Sammy's federal program. Here is their contact information:

U.S. Department of Education
www.ed.gov
800-4-FED-AID

Sallie Mae
www.salliemae.com
888-2-SALLIE

Repayment Programs

Both the U.S. Department of Education and Sallie Mae have their own version of repayment schedules. Here is a basic overview of each one.

Standard Repayment Plan. This plan requires you to pay a fixed amount each month (at least $50) for up to ten years. The length of your actual repayment period will depend on your loan amount.

Extended Repayment Plan. This plan allows you to extend loan repayment over a period that is generally twelve to thirty years, depending on your loan amount. Your monthly payment may be lower than it would be if you repaid the same total loan amount of interest over the life of your loan, because the repayment period may be longer. The minimum monthly payment is $50.

Graduated Repayment Plan. This plan means that your payments will be lower at first and then will increase, typically every two years. The length of your repayment period will generally range from twelve to thirty years, depending on your loan amount. Your monthly payment may range from 50 to 150 percent of what it would be if you were repaying the same total loan amount under the Standard Repayment Plan. However, you'll repay a higher total amount of interest because the repayment period is longer than it is under the Standard Repayment Plan.

Income Contingent Plan. This plan bases your monthly payment on your yearly income, family size, and loan amount. As your income rises or falls, so do your payments. After twenty-five years, any remaining balance on the loan will be forgiven, but you may have to pay taxes on the amount forgiven.

Having difficulty coming up with the dough each month?

If you have trouble making your student loan repayments, you may qualify for one of the following forms of payment relief:

Deferment. With deferment you have the right to defer repayment for certain defined periods. A deferment is a temporary suspension of loan payments for specific situations, such as returning to school, unemployment, disability, or military service.

Forbearance. This is a temporary postponement or reduction of payments for a period of time, the length of which you and the lender or holder of your loan may agree to, because you are experiencing financial difficulty.

Other Forms of Payment Relief. Graduated and income-sensitive payment plans are available. Graduated payment plans provide short-term relief through low interest-only payments followed by standard principal and interest payments. An income-sensitive payment plan offers borrowers payment relief with payments that are a percentage of the borrower's gross monthly income.

These alternatives can provide you with credit relief and help you maintain a good credit rating, so please remember that it is important to take action before you incur late fees or roll the dice on damaging your credit rating by not making payments on your student loans.

Lifetime Learning Credit

Don't forget about the federal government's educational tax credit. The Internal Revenue Service currently offers a tax credit for higher educational expenses that will help reduce your tax liability. The Lifetime Learning Credit is a tax credit equal to 20 percent of your tuition expenses, up to $5,000, for virtually any postsecondary education and training. This includes expenses related to a course of instruction or other education that involves sports, games, hobbies, or other noncredit courses that are considered eligible if they are part of a course of instruction to acquire or improve job skills. To find out more information on claiming this tax credit, you can get a copy of Publication 970 by calling or visiting the IRS Web site at *www.irs.ustreas.gov/prod/forms_pubs/* (800-829-3676).

> **Pay the Highest Rate Off First!**
>
> If you have both types of debt (credit card and student loan) discussed in this chapter, chances are you are paying a lower rate of interest on your student loan debt. And as you can see from the information we just discussed on both types of debt, student loan debt offers much more flexibility as far as paying it back. If, in fact, your credit card debt interest is higher, make a plan to pay it off first.
>
> How can you do this? Try to reduce your monthly payment on your student loans to free up some extra cash each month to put toward paying off your credit card debt. When you have finished paying off your credit card debt, increase your student loan's monthly payment plan back to its original level.

Pay It Forward

Another neat option to consider is a program run by a non-profit called Americorps. They provide full-time educational awards in return for work in community service—in other words, "pay it forward." You can work before, during, or after your postsecondary education, and you can use the funds either to pay current educational expenses or to repay federal student loans. For more information on this program, contact Americorps at *www.americorps.org* (800-942-2677).

Knowing Your Options

As you can see, there are many ways to gear up budget lean and debt free. Respecting yourself enough to take time out from your hectic life to figure out exactly where you stand financially and how much you owe is huge. And please keep in mind that you can apply these tools to every aspect of your life. You simply have to break it down and decide what's most important to you. You deserve another big hug and congratulations. Way to be and way to go!

Switchback Terrain

- Be budget lean! Take the time to respect yourself and your money. What do you truly weigh on the money scale? Calculate exactly how much it costs you to live each month after your taxes have been taken into consideration.
- Be budget savvy! Make a detailed budget spreadsheet either on Microsoft Excel or simple notebook paper. List all expenses for each month. Be sure to review and update your monthly expenses.

- Cut back on what you spend.
  1. Wait twenty-four hours before spending $100 or more.
  2. Track what you spend.
  3. Pay cash.
  4. Nix a few credit cards.
- If you have credit card debt, consolidate your debt onto the card offering the lowest rate of interest available in the market. Map out a monthly payment plan to pay off your debt as soon as possible.
- If you've already established good credit for yourself, nix all your credit cards and use an ATM debit card instead. If you feel uncomfortable without a credit card, make sure you get the best deal possible and pay the bill as soon as it arrives!
- If you have student loans, you have options available to you that offer ways to lower your monthly interest payment, consolidate them into one loan, and even defer payment if you are unable to come up with the cash to meet monthly payments now.
- Be sure not to default on your student loan; doing so is serious business that could result in the federal government, among other entities, taking action against you to recover the money, including notifying national credit bureaus of your default.

chapter 4

Three Adventure Backpacks to Go, Please!

"Because of our routines
we forget that life is an ongoing
adventure."
—**Maya Angelou**

In this chapter I will show you other essential tools you will absolutely need on the money trail. You will learn how to equip yourself with three essential adventure backpacks: funds for emergency, retirement, and dreams. If you fill these backpacks properly with savvy financial investment gear (we will talk more about investment gear in Chapter 5), you can map out a financial life filled with health, wealth, and good fun!

Your emergency adventure backpack will be your floating device should you accidentally take a tumble off the money trail and land in a turbulent river of financial troubles. Your retirement adventure backpack will offer you the ability to make a strong Uncle Sam–less (read tax-deferred) investment in yourself for the very long future you have ahead of you. Last, your dream adventure backpack will offer you a way to make all of the possibilities of your life's desires a reality.

Preparing and Packing Your Emergency Adventure Backpack

Think of your *emergency* adventure backpack as an inflatable life raft available to you any time you experience some unexpected near-term financial hardship, such as having your car break down or losing your job. Your emergency adventure backpack will keep you afloat, ensuring a safe, quasipeaceful ride down the river of distress to a safer place. In other words, you will not be left flailing about in choppy waters!

In your emergency adventure backpack you will need to sock away three to six months' worth of "scratch" (my teenage brother's slang for money) to meet your basic living expenses. How much cash you ultimately pack into your emergency adventure backpack depends first on how you approach preparing for challenges. How do you prepare for a tough, long hike? Are you the kind of girl who takes extra care to eat well and go to bed early the day before? Or are you the kind of girl who burns the midnight oil, clubbing into the wee hours of the night? As you probably guessed, if you're the type to plan cautiously, then six months' worth of cash is what you will want to pack. On the other hand, if you're comfortable living a little more on the edge (and with less sleep), perhaps three months would work just fine for you.

Second, you will need to consider how difficult it would be to replace your current income stream, meaning, how long would it take you to get another job that pays your current salary? Is it two months or six months? If the latter, consider packing six months' worth of cash in your emergency adventure backpack. Keep in mind, if you're a high roller raking in the big bucks at your current job, you may want to play it safe and plan for packing away six months' worth of cash in your emergency adventure backpack. Why? Because the more you make, the more you will need to replace should you lose your job.

We all need an emergency adventure backpack—how big or small is up to who we are individually. And since your emergency adventure backpack will be created with reserve cash, it will need to be ready for release in a bind. Consider stashing this cash in a money market checking account (which I will discuss below in more detail). Remember, there's no right or wrong way to pack cash into your emergency adventure backpack.

Backwoods Banking

In today's economy, a typical checking or savings account at a bank will offer you *at best* a rate of interest on your money between 0 and 2 percent. With these types of accounts, you can also plan on being charged monthly bank fees just for having the account. Think about this for a minute. You're giving the bank your hard-earned money only to lose it back to inflation because when you take inflation (4 percent average annual rate) into consideration, you're losing money each year on simply putting your money into one of these accounts.

In effect, you are lending the bank your money, which they will use for their own profit, yet they are charging you a fee just for the privilege of having an account with them. Even worse, they're paying you a truly crappy rate of return. Sounds like good business for them and very bad business for you.

Money Market Accounts

The solution to this problem is a money market checking account. Most brokerage and mutual fund firms, plus banks, offer money market checking accounts that pay competitive interest rates. As of this writing, these types of accounts are paying depositors approximately 5 percent a year (which beats inflation). That is significant considering that the average bank checking account rate is around 1 percent. The major difference between bank checking accounts versus money market checking accounts is that the federal government backs the former through the Federal Deposit Insurance Corporation (FDIC). Not to worry, the U.S. Securities and Exchange Commission closely regulates money market checking accounts. Never has the money market funds industry caused an individual to lose even a penny of principal.

Plus, with money market checking accounts you can get an ATM debit card, unlimited check-writing privileges with no monthly fee, and no minimum balance to maintain. Unbelievable! Think we're talking small potatoes when considering all of these little fees and rates of interest? Take a look at this example:

Checking Account vs. Money Market Account:	
Checking or savings account @ 1% annual interest	$5,000 @ 1% = **$50**
Money market account @ 5% annual interest	$5,000 @ 5% = **$250**

And don't forget to consider the bank fees you're charged just for having an account. Oh, and perhaps they offer you an ATM bank card that costs $1 for every transaction over four each month. You could be looking at as much as $60 in bank fees and another $40 in ATM transactions per year. With a money market account you not only save these fees, you can earn a competitive interest rate on your money. Remember, a little here and a little there add up!

You will need to shop around at the different banks, brokerages, and mutual fund firms in your area to find the best offer on obtaining a money market account. Here are a few questions you will want to ask to determine the best money market account for you.

- **What is the minimum amount I need to open the account?** "Zero" is the answer you're looking for.
- **What is the minimum balance required to keep the account open?** "Zero" is the answer you're looking for.
- **Is there a yearly fee to have this account?** "No" is the answer you're looking for.
- **Do I need to purchase securities to maintain the account? If I don't plan to, will you charge me a fee? If so, how often?** Many money market accounts require

you to make a minimum of one to three transactions per annum to avoid annual fee charges to your account. By transaction I mean buying or selling a stock or mutual fund, or any other type of security. This is not a big deal. In any event, the fee is typically very small, like $10. Plus, this may encourage you to finally pick up that stock you've talked about buying for a year now!

If this makes you really nervous, the answer you are looking for is "No."

- **Do you issue an ATM debit card?** The answer should be "Yes."
- **Do you charge a fee when I use the ATM?** The answer should be "No."
- **Is there a maximum number of checks that I can write each month?** The answer should be "No."
- **Is there a minimum amount for which checks can be written?** The answer should be "No."
- **What interest rate are you currently paying?** The higher the better!
- **How do you credit this interest?** Each day is what you want to hear.

Disability Disconnect

I know what you're thinking: *disability what?* Most of us young pups don't really give much thought to injury or illness that we may incur. But this is the time to give disability insurance a little thought. Disability is a type of insurance you may want to consider buying for your emergency adventure backpack. It can protect you in case of a catastrophe, by which I mean an illness, injury, or chronic condition that would prevent you from working and earning an income for an extended period of time. It is a type of insurance for the "what-if" scenarios in your life. Disability insurance differs from workers' compensation because it protects you from any illness or injury whether it happens at home, on the job, or on vacation. Workers' comp only protects you from injury you may incur while on the job.

According to the *Disability Management Sourcebook*, the number of people between seventeen and forty-four with severe disabilities has increased 400 percent over the past twenty-five years.

One in seven people will become disabled for five years or more before they reach sixty-five!

Plus, because we have more years to live than our elders, we have a greater possibility of being disabled. The table below shows the odds of a person having at least one long-term disability (three months or longer) before reaching age sixty-five.

Age	Disability
25	44%
30	42%
35	41%
40	39%
45	36%
50	33%
55	27%

Women, in fact, tend to incur more disabling factors and have a higher incidence of claim rate than men due to miscarriages, hysterectomies, and the like. Given the strong probability statistically that you could lose your earnings power through disability, you need to be smart and protect yourself now.

Most disability plans offer 60 to 70 percent of your gross income (that's before taxes) to be paid out to you monthly four to six months after you are disabled. At this writing, however, only five states offer disability insurance benefits: California, Hawaii, New Jersey, New York, and Rhode Island, plus Puerto Rico. If your employer offers you disability insurance that they will pay for on your behalf, be aware that you will be taxed on the 60- to 70-percent-of-salary disability benefits you receive from them. Keep in mind that this after-tax number may mean you don't have enough to meet your monthly living expenses.

Individual Coverage

One thing you can do to keep this shortfall from happening is to request individual coverage in addition to what your employer offers you from a disability insurance provider. The good news here is that based on your age, you can lock into a rate that will hold steady until you are sixty-five. And the younger you are, the cheaper the lock-in rate! Here is a list of disability insurance providers you may want to contact:

Disability Insurance Services specializes in offering competitive quotes from disability insurance companies such as Standard, Guardian, Berkshire, Pan American, Fidelity Security, Mass Mutual, and Lloyd's of London. Contact them at *www.diexpert.com* (800-898-9641).

Unum Provident
www.unum.com
800-843-3426

USAA Insurance
www.usaa.com
800-531-8000

When shopping around for a good policy or obtaining individual coverage in addition to group coverage, here are a few good questions to ask.

- **What percentage of income will the policy pay?** As mentioned, most pay 60 to 70 percent of your current salary. The higher the percentage, the higher the rate… normally. Be sure to ask the cap on what they will pay. Many companies have a cap of $5,000 per month.

- **How long is the waiting (elimination) period?** The waiting period is the time between when you're disabled and when you receive your first disability benefit payment. This period is known in official terms as the elimination period. Typically, the time frame is three to six months, but you may be able to lower your rate by extending the waiting period to eight months. This only makes sense if

1. you have enough savings to tide you over through the additional delay
2. your employer is willing to pay you a salary in the early months of your disability
3. this is the only way you can afford coverage

- **How long is the benefits period?** Your benefits period begins the moment you start receiving disability payouts. If you ever become disabled, you don't continue to pay a premium. Many companies pay disability benefits until the employee reaches sixty-five.

- **Will you cover me if I am disabled because of illness as well as accident?** The answer should be "Yes."

- **Do you offer residual benefits?** You will want a policy that will pay you according to how much you can work based on the disability you incur. For example, if you can only work 50 percent of what you did prior to being disabled, you will want 50 percent of your disability benefits.

- **How long will the policy cover me?** You want the policy to cover you up until you are sixty-five.

- **Is the policy portable, meaning you can take it with you when you leave and continue it under your own name?** Should you choose to leave your company, the policy you purchase must be portable.

- **Is the policy guaranteed renewable?** The answer should be "Yes."

- Is the policy "Owner's OCC" or is it "Any OCC"? "Owner's OCC" will pay you if you can't perform your specific job. "Any OCC" will pay you only if you are disabled and can't perform any job. Obviously you are looking for "Owner's OCC."

Be smart; make sure you pack disability insurance in your emergency adventure backpack!

Preparing and Packing Your Retirement Adventure Backpack

Building and funding your *retirement* adventure backpack is one of the best ways to ensure you summit the money trail with ease and success. Your retirement adventure backpack is a core piece of equipment when it comes to healthy long-term financial planning. Even though we discussed your emergency adventure backpack first, that doesn't mean you should put off funding your retirement adventure backpack. Ideally, you should build both backpacks simultaneously.

Put Yourself First

What do I mean by putting yourself first? I mean you must begin to put yourself ahead of everybody else when it comes to dishing out those monthly expense payments! Think about this: you put Uncle Sammy, your landlord, your credit card company, and many others first every month by paying them before paying wonderful, amazing you! Yuck!

I want you to take 10 percent from your gross income each month and begin packing it into your retirement adventure backpack. You have many different choices available to you. One of the best ways to help make a dent in the "Putting Yourself First" plan is through pre-tax retirement accounts.

Pre-Tax Retirement Accounts

Pre-tax retirement accounts are retirement accounts that allow you to deposit a portion of your gross income before accounting for federal, state, and local taxes. Let's say you made $50,000 this year and managed to contribute 10 percent to your company's 401(k) plan. You have accomplished two very significant things. To begin with, you have put yourself first and reduced your taxable gross income by $5,000 to $45,000. If you are in the 28 percent federal tax bracket and in the 10 percent state tax bracket, you have saved $1,400 in federal taxes and $500 in state taxes. If you didn't put this money away, you would really only get to spend $3,200 after paying your taxes.

Second, when you put your money into a pre-tax retirement account, 100 percent of that money goes to work for you. As long as this money stays in a pre-tax retirement account, it will go to work for you without any outside interruption from Uncle Sammy, or anyone else for that matter!

Year	401(k) Yearly Contribution	Interest Earned at 10% per Annum
1	$6,000	$600
2	$6,000	$1,260
3	$6,000	$1,986
4	$6,000	$2,784
5	$6,000	$3,663
6	$6,000	$4,629
7	$6,000	$5,692
8	$6,000	$6,861
9	$6,000	$8,147
10	$6,000	$9,562
11	$6,000	$11,118
12	$6,000	$12,830
13	$6,000	$14,713
14	$6,000	$16,784
15	$6,000	$19,062
16	$6,000	$21,569
17	$6,000	$24,326
18	$6,000	$27,358
19	$6,000	$30,694
20	$6,000	$34,363

Compounding Coolness

Remember when we chatted in Chapter 1 about time being on your side and what that can do for your money if invested? Well, when you invest your money in a tax-deferred retirement account you allow it to multiply over time through the power of compound interest. Compound interest will be key in summiting your money trail. Not sure? Look at the sample chart preceding page: if you made a $6,000 per annum investment in your 401(k), how long would it take before your interest added up to more than your initial contribution?

At year eight, your interest earned equals more than your annual contribution to the retirement plan. At year twelve, your interest earned is equal to more than double your annual contribution to the retirement plan. Finally, at year seventeen, your interest earned is equal to more than *quadruple* your annual contribution to the plan! This chart clearly illustrates the coolness of compounding. Remember, the higher the rate of return, the higher your compound interest capabilities will be to grow your money over time. So give yourself time *and* compound interest when it comes to your financial planning, especially your retirement planning.

There are only two pre-tax retirement accounts, the employer-sponsored plan, which your company provides for you, and the individual plan, which you provide for yourself. Due to corporate restructuring, downsizing, or the possibility of working for yourself one day, you should familiarize yourself with both of these plans and how exactly they work.

Employer-Sponsored Retirement Plans

Employer-sponsored retirement plans are offered through employers and are normally free to join. If you haven't joined your company's plan yet, call your benefits department in human resources ASAP and find out if you're eligible. If so, let them know that you would like to sign up immediately. There is normally a waiting period of twelve months after arrival at a company before you are eligible to participate in its plan.

What are the different types of employer-sponsored plans?

401(k). This is the most popular retirement plan offered through employers. Its name was taken from its dedicated section in the federal tax code. You can usually contribute up to approximately 15 percent of your salary to the plan.

403(b). This plan acts just like a 401(k). It was set up for nonprofit organizations such as universities, hospitals, and research organizations.

SIMPLE. This plan was put into place on January 1, 1997, for companies that employ one hundred or fewer employees. The acronym stands for *savings incentive match plan for employees.* The rules for contribution and withdrawal are a little different than with the 401(k) or 403(b), but the same basic concepts apply.

How much can you put into your plan?

The government has rules and regulations regarding this. For the year 2001, you are allowed to put up to $10,500 in a 401(k) and 403(b) in one year. For SIMPLEs, it's $6,500. These numbers are tied directly to inflation and will rise in line with it. For example, if inflation is 4 percent this year, you can expect a $420 ($10,500 x 4 percent) increase in your 401(k) contribution limit.

How do you put money into the plan?

Once you decide how much you want to put into the plan per month, that amount will be automatically deducted from your paycheck before the various taxing authorities take their 40 percent plus (typically) bite. Remember, this money will be invested *all for you*, without interference from Uncle Sammy. You absolutely need to max out—meaning contribute the maximum allowable amount to—your employer-sponsored retirement plan. Maxing out is a great way to help you finish hiking the money trail rich.

What is "matching" all about?

In some cases, employers will supplement your retirement plan contributions with contributions of their own. This means your employer may choose to offer you matching contributions to your plan, anywhere from 10 to 100 percent of your contribution. Let's say you work for a company that offers you a 20 percent matching contribution. That means if you contribute $5,000 from your annual compensation to the plan in one year, your employer will add another $1,000 (20 percent of your contribution) to the plan.

This is a fantastic perk. It's like getting free money for doing something that's great for you. Talk about putting yourself first! Even if your employer doesn't match your contribution, be sure to try to max out your full allowable contribution to the plan. I've had other young women tell me, "My employer only matches 20 percent of what I put in the plan, so I'm only going to put in 20 percent of what I am allowed. If they aren't going to put in 100 percent, why should I?" Ugh! This isn't about punishing your employer. Ultimately, you are the only one who will benefit from the plan. Remember, maxing out your plan is the single most effective way for you to become financially secure for your future. You have the ability to amass millions of dollars because you are still young. All you have to do is one simple thing: make sure you put as much as possible in these plans.

Where does my money go?

The company administering the plan invests your money for you. There are three basic types of investment options that you will have to consider:

- Do I want to invest in my company's stock?
- Do I want to invest in the stock market through mutual funds?
- Do I want to invest in an investment vehicle, such as a bond, that will offer me a guaranteed fixed rate of return?

How do I choose the investment options in my plan?

Extremely carefully. This will probably be one of the most important decisions you will ever make on your money journey! I suggest you review all of the information given to you about the available investments in your plan and then find a qualified financial advisor guide (in Chapter 5 I will review how to find the right financial advisor guide for you) to discuss them with. Should you decide to change your selection at any time after you are invested, you can. Most plans allow you to change your selection from one investment in the plan to another. However, the option to make a change may only be made available to plan participants once or twice a year.

Should I invest in my company's stock?

As a loyal employee, it's natural to want to support your company through buying shares in it. However, keep in mind that tying up your money in one stock is risky. Your retirement plan is for the long haul, and you want to diversify your investments as much as possible. You can invest a little in your own firm, but spread your money around to make sure you're protected in case anything happens to your company's stock. Keep in mind that company policy differs, and you will need to check with your company to see how many times you can change your holdings per year. As noted above, typically it is once or twice.

When can I get my money out of my retirement plan?

You will need to check the plan summary description, which is available through your human resources office. Typically you can begin withdrawing your money from the plan at age fifty-nine-and-a-half. If you think you might need to get at your retirement stash early, talk with a tax accountant first.

Can you take your retirement plan with you?

If you leave your present company you can either leave the money in the original plan (if you have at least $5,000 in the account, generally), where it will continue to grow, or you can "roll over" your plan (no minimum amount required) either to a new employer's plan or to a new IRA (individual retirement account) of your own. Keep in mind that it may be advantageous to roll over the plan because you will have more options with which to control the funds, as these options often disappear if you are no longer an employee. If you do this correctly, the government will not consider this transfer of funds a withdrawal, and as such you will not have to pay penalties or taxes.

> "Whatever you can do or dream you can, begin it. Boldness has genius, magic, and power in it. Begin it now."
> —Goethe

Individual Retirement Plans

The three different types of individual retirement plans are traditional IRAs, Roth IRAs, and SEP IRAs.

What are IRAs?

IRAs are individual retirement accounts that are set up for employees who work for companies that do not offer retirement plans or for self-employed people who need a type of retirement plan to which to contribute.

If you contribute to your company's plan, are you still eligible to contribute to an IRA?

Yes, you may be eligible to contribute to a traditional IRA or a Roth IRA.

Traditional IRAs and Roth IRAs

Just like your employer-sponsored retirement plan, if the money stays in your traditional or Roth IRA, it can grow tax deferred. Contributions to a traditional IRA may be deductible, but contributions to a Roth IRA are never deductible. I will show you the upside of Roth IRAs on the next page, but for now I'm listing the two basic rules for both.

- Anyone who earns an annual income from a job and is under the age of seventy-and-a-half is eligible to contribute up to $2,000 per year to a traditional or a Roth IRA.

- If eligible, you may only contribute to one plan per year. This means you contribute up to $2,000 to a traditional *or* a Roth IRA, not to both in one year!

Here are a couple of important features of traditional and Roth IRAs:

- You can begin to draw your money out of your traditional IRA at age fifty-nine-and-a-half. Taking money out before then means you will incur a 10 percent penalty from the federal and state levels and be taxed on the amount of withdrawal as ordinary income. This penalty does not apply if you qualify (in certain circumstances) and are using the money to pay college bills, pay health insurance fees, buy your first home, pay long-term disability costs, or cover medical emergencies.

- You can begin to draw your money out of your Roth IRA at age fifty-nine-and-a-half. However, you may also draw the principal investment amount out any time prior to that without being penalized. The only thing you can't do is take out the interest you earned from your investment in the plan prior to age fifty-nine-and-a-half. Please note, however, once you remove the money from your Roth IRA, you *cannot* put it back into the plan.

- If you did not take a tax deduction on your original contributions to your traditional IRA, when you are eligible to draw from it you will only be taxed on the earnings and growth that investment made over the years, not on your original investment

- If you do not have an employer-sponsored plan, the entire contribution of $2,000 to your traditional IRA is tax deductible. If you contribute to your employer-sponsored plan, you may still be eligible to make tax-deductible contributions to an IRA. How much is fully deductible depends on the size of your income.

Currently, these are the rules that preclude you from taking an IRA tax deduction:

- If you are single and your adjusted gross income is more than $41,000.
- If you are married, you file a joint tax return, and your adjusted gross income is more than $61,000 combined.
- If you are married but file separately and your adjusted gross income is more than $10,000.

Currently, these are the rules that may make you eligible for a partial tax deduction:

- If you are single and your adjusted gross income is less than $41,000.
- If you are married, you file a joint tax return, and your adjusted gross income is less than $61,000 combined.
- If you are married but file separately and your adjusted gross income is less than $10,000.

I Beg to Differ, Sir!

As I mentioned earlier, the major difference between a Roth IRA and a traditional IRA is that with a Roth IRA, not only does your money have the ability to grow in the plan tax-deferred (like a traditional IRA), but when you go to take your money out (drum roll, please), you will not be taxed on a single penny of what you've earned from the growth. And, one more time for the record, even if you contribute to an employer-sponsored plan, you may still qualify to deduct your $2,000 traditional IRA contribution. Your $2,000 Roth IRA contribution is *never* tax deductible.

When it comes to making a choice between a Roth IRA and a traditional IRA you should think of it as a type of exchange. What's worth more to you? The $2,000 tax deduction you will get in the current year from a traditional IRA, or the money you will save much later down the road by never having to pay taxes on your Roth IRA withdrawals when you choose to retire?

Financial planners advise that those who are more than ten to fifteen years away from retirement (that's us, hiker girls), choose a Roth IRA. Why? Age. Our age translates into more time. And with more time the benefits of hunky tax-free distribution much later down the road definitely outweigh the benefits of a tax deduction now.

SEP IRAs

SEP stands for Simplified Employee Pension Plan, and SEP IRAs are a great way for entrepreneurs to put themselves first because the maximum allowable contribution to the plan per annum is high, $25,500 for the year 2001. To qualify for a SEP IRA you must be self-employed, own a small business, or participate in a small partnership. This type of retirement plan is very easy to set up, while the regulations and rules of distribution and withdrawal are very much like those that govern traditional and Roth IRAs and 401(k)s.

With a SEP IRA you can contribute up to 13.043 percent (again, year 2001) of your annual income if you are filing with the IRS as a self-employed individual (meaning you fill out the IRS form called "Schedule C") and the monies you put into the plan will be treated as a tax-deductible contribution. If you are a small-business owner or are involved with a small partnership, you may make a 15 percent tax-deductible contribution of your employees' annual compensation to the plan.

If you are currently self-employed, don't miss out on this awesome opportunity to set up one of these pups! It's as simple as a phone call or e-mail to your broker, financial planner, or bank. Once it's set up, you will be on your way to a brighter path on the money trail and to actively putting yourself first.

Be Pre-Tax Retirement Investment Wise

Hopefully by this point you have identified how much you will contribute to your retirement plan and decided what retirement account would work best for you. Earlier in the chapter we discussed that if you are enrolled in your employer-sponsored retirement plan, you most likely have about five investment options available to you. Please note that your investment options may broaden even more if you participate in any of the IRAs discussed earlier. If you contribute to a plan, and I know you will, you will have investment options such as stocks, mutual funds, and bonds, all of which we will discuss in Chapter 5.

Don't Play the Fool!

Many people mistakenly think that once they have identified how much they will contribute to their retirement plan and which type of plan to invest in, then *basta*, they're done! Nope. The most important part of this entire process is just about to begin. Now you need to choose where your contribution will go. So please remember to take these three important steps with your retirement plans:

⊙ Decide which one is right for you.

⊙ Put money in the plan.

⊙ Inform your plan administrator, bank, brokerage firm, or financial advisor as to how you want the money you put into the plan to be invested.

As silly as this may sound, when it comes to the choices you make with your retirement plan or plans, these decisions are as important as deciding whether to marry, move, or change jobs. Think I'm kidding? Think again!

TRAIL TALE...

I heard this compelling and true story at a local financial seminar. Two women, Sally and Ann, worked for an electric company. Both women had worked for the company for the same period of time, thirty years. Thirty years earlier, Sally and Ann had been given forms to fill out regarding their employer-sponsored retirement plan. Both women had been asked by the plan administrator in their human resources department to choose which investment their future contributions would go toward. Sally checked the growth (stocks) box and Ann checked the income (bonds) box.

Due to corporate downsizing thirty years after they had been hired, Sally and Ann were laid off at the same time. Guess who had more money? Sally! Her employer-sponsored retirement account grew to more than $925,000. Ann, however, was not so lucky. Her plan was worth only $352,000, which made the very big difference between Sally having the option to retire after she was laid off and Ann needing to seek other employment opportunities.

Don't be like Ann! After all, you work hard to make the money you contribute to your retirement plan. Don't you deserve to have that money work just as hard for you? Don't joke around when you're filling out retirement plan forms. Focus carefully on how you will allocate your funds and on choosing the best investment options available for you.

Preparing and Packing Your Dream Adventure Backpack

What do I mean by *dream* adventure backpack? Well, something along the lines of money stashed away for a wild fancy! Or how about having the ability to imagine something as possible or conceivable? Your dream adventure backpack could be as simple as a goal or an aim. Take a moment to think about your inner child. Begin to imagine her in all of her innocence. What comes to mind? What dreams does she have?

Have you always wanted to explore the world? Take a safari to Africa? Perhaps your dream is to quit your job and devote all of your time to the homeless in America. You could want to run your own business, start a magazine, or adopt a baby on your own. Your dream adventure backpack is there to make sure you keep doing something that's really important: dreaming!

Hitting the money trail should mean that you create a way to keep dreaming. How do you do that? You make sure that you've packed enough money into your dream adventure back-pack to make your dreams become a reality.

The ability to dream exists in each and every one of us. We just get so caught up with our hectic days that we sometimes forget to take a few moments to sit quietly and dream. Take a minute now to offer yourself a time-out. Go for a walk around the neighborhood, sip a cup of coffee at a nearby cafe, or just stretch out on your couch. It's okay. You're allowed to do this. Or are you the kind of girl who finds it difficult to do nothing? Well, you're not alone. Most of us find comfort in being busy. And let's face it, we live in a society where being busy is common behavior for most folks.

"Reach for your dreams and
they will reach for you."
—Hana Rosa Zadra

But this is your moment to take a breather to explore your inner world. What comes up for you? What excites you? All you need to do to make your dreams a reality is

- identify what they are
- create an investment plan to finance them

If you're not sure what your dreams are yet, or what exactly you would like to add to your dream adventure backpack, that's okay, too. You're not being graded or tested in this book. As your guide, I seek to offer you the concepts and tools on how to think and "be" with your money. A dream of yours could be to travel around the world, study Buddhism, or even design your own home. Keep saying to yourself, "I wish for _____." Remember to give yourself some time to reflect. The answers will come, I promise.

> "Dreams are illustrations...from the book of your soul writing about you."
> —Marsha Norman

Where Do I Put My Dream Adventure Backpack Money?

Where you decide to put your money will depend on whether your dreams are for the short view or the long view. We will discuss more about your short-view and long-view investment gear options in the next chapter. For now, keep in mind that your dream adventure backpack will work just like your emergency and retirement adventure backpacks. Once you decide what your dream is, how much it will cost, and which time frame it fits—short view or long view—you will need to make sure you develop a plan to fund it each month.

> "What do you pack to pursue a dream
> and what do you leave behind?"
> **—Sandra Sharpe**

If you are like many women, funding your dream adventure backpack may not be a top priority. Perhaps your emergency and retirement backpacks take precedence. And hey, I totally understand. Since I started my own hike on the money trail I've taken plenty of time to get all three of my adventure backpacks together. And quite frankly, doing so will always be a work in progress.

If you are in a similar situation, this doesn't mean you can't fund your dream adventure backpack just a little bit. Try just 1 percent of your monthly income, or put aside just fifty bucks a month, for example. Something is better than nothing. So don't forget to begin a "Wish List" and start funding your dream adventure backpack. I hope you know by now that because of time and compound interest, a little can go a long way!

Now that you know how to equip yourself with your adventure backpacks, time to learn how to choose savvy investment gear for your short-term, mid-term, and long-term investment options. Follow me to the next chapter!

Switchback Terrain

The money trail will require three adventure backpacks equipped to fit you just right.

- **Emergency Adventure Backpack.** Think of your emergency adventure backpack as an inflatable raft available to you at any time in case you experience some unexpected near-term financial hardship, such as having your car break down or losing your job. You will need to pack three to six months' worth of living expenses into this backpack, plus disability insurance in case of a catastrophe such as an illness, injury, or chronic condition that would prevent you from working for an extended period of time.

- **Retirement Adventure Backpack.** Creating and funding your retirement adventure backpack is one of the best ways to put yourself first and successfully summit the money trail. It is imperative that you max out your employer-sponsored retirement plan and participate in contributing to an IRA and, if self-employed, open a SEP IRA. The younger you are, the easier it is to amass great chunks of dough through systematic investment plans that offer you the amazing power of compound interest.

- **Dream Adventure Backpack.** Dare to dream and dare to live that dream! With your dream adventure backpack as your resource, your hopes, wishes, and fantasies have the chance to mark your life with great wonderment and bliss.

A few examples of dreams are to

1. travel around the world

2. start your own business

3. design your own home

All you need to do to make your dreams a reality is identify them and create an investment plan to finance them.

chapter 5

Be a Trailblazer with Savvy Investment Gear

"Your vision will become
clear only when you can look into
your own heart."
—**Carl Jung**

hen I say your adventure backpacks need to be filled with different types of investment gear, what exactly do I mean? I mean money market accounts, CDs (certificates of deposit), stocks, mutual funds, and bonds. My goal is for you to get the most out of your money, and that means utilizing all available investment options. Now that you know what you need to think about packing in your adventure backpacks and how tax-deferred retirement investing works (as we discussed in Chapter 4), it's time to identify the best investment gear for you to pack into them. There are several ways to create harmony, balance, and consistency within your portfolio as your money grows. This applies even if all you start with is $100—hey, everybody has to start somewhere!

Investment Gear
for the Short View

When hiking for the short view you need to equip yourself with investment gear that's low risk and allows you to quickly access your money at any time along the way. The short-view hike has a duration time of one month to two years. Your investment gear options will include

1. money market accounts

2. CDs

3. U.S. Treasury bills

Money Market Accounts
(or, Money for Nothing and
Your Checks for Free...)

Money market accounts are similar to savings accounts: They act like a mutual fund that invests in short-term securities (which are usually U.S. Treasury bills). For every dollar you put in you get a dollar back, plus the interest your money earns from the investments the fund makes. Since these funds are essentially risk free, some investors prefer them to stocks or bond funds. I've already discussed at length the benefits of using money market accounts as opposed to checking or savings accounts, but if you need a refresher, please flip back to Chapter 4 and have another quick read.

Certificates of Deposit

CDs are a type of bond that is issued by a bank. With a CD, as with any bond, you agree to lend your money to an organization such as a bank or brokerage firm for a predetermined number of months or years. The idea is that the longer you decide to lock up your money, the higher the interest rate you receive. A CD deposit can range from $500 to $100,000, and these certain periods can be as short as one month or as long as ten years. At the time of this writing, rates were going for around 5 percent. Unlike the money market accounts, CDs are federally insured for up to $100,000. That's the good news!

The bad news is that if you need to get at your stash before your CD matures, you will have to pay a penalty costing you up to as much as half of the interest you were supposed to earn. This is why you should nix the CD if you can find a money market account that offers a better rate of interest.

Treasury Bills

Treasury bills, also known as T-bills, are another type of bond, or fixed-income security, issued by the federal government, with a maturity of one year or less. T-bills can be purchased in a few ways; you may buy them directly from the U.S. Treasury Department, a bank, or a brokerage firm. But get this: one bill costs $10,000. And T-bills don't typically pay interest.

So why in the world would you buy one? Well, like many other bonds, T-bills are issued at a discount and then redeemed at full price when they mature. It would be like buying a dress at 25 percent off, returning it, and then getting a refund for the full price of the dress. (Wall Street calls this "par value.")

For example, if the one-year T-bill rate happens to be 5 percent, you would pay $9,500 for a certificate that you could redeem for $10,000 one year later. Still not clear? Let me try to help.

There are three main reasons why people like T-bills:

1. They are backed by the full faith of the U.S. government, and it just doesn't get safer than that.

2. They are exempt from state tax, meaning the state cannot tax you on the money you make from this investment.

3. If you buy your T-bill from a brokerage firm, they can normally be sold ASAP so you can collect your money within three days. There is no penalty for selling your T-bill before it matures, but expect a smaller redemption. And keep in mind that you might also have to pay a commission to your broker.

Investment Gear for the Long View

When hiking for the long view you need to equip yourself with investment gear that is of greater risk, thus offering you higher growth. Remember, when it comes to investing, higher risk usually will mean higher reward (growth). Your hiking duration for the long view will be two to ten years or more, and your investment gear will include

1. bonds
2. stocks
3. mutual funds

Bonding with Bonds

We discussed earlier that a bond is a loan you make to an issuer, usually a corporation or the government. The issuer of the bond specifies when you will be paid back (Wall Street calls it a "maturity date"). How much interest you will earn in the interim is usually paid in two installments a year. The most important measure you will need to remember with bonds is this: the higher the rating, the lower the interest rate you will receive. Less risk equals lower rate of return.

Bonds are typically issued in increments of $1,000, $5,000, or $10,000, and time to maturity (when you can cash in your chips, or bonds) can be as short as one year and as long as thirty years, depending on the type of bond. With the exception of U.S. savings bonds, few are sold for less than $1,000. Keep in mind that with bonds, the shorter the time period to maturity, the less risk for bond buyers of getting paid their principal from the bond issuer.

There are hundreds of different types of bonds available. They range from super-safe government savings bonds to high-yield bonds, also known as junk bonds. For example, companies that might go bust are high risk and offer a better rate of return (Wall Street calls these "high yield"). If you buy government bonds, you will earn less interest but your money is safe. To keep it simple, I suggest you restrict your bond buying to the following categories:

1. Treasury notes and bonds
2. corporate bonds
3. municipal bonds

Treasury Notes and Bonds

Treasury notes and bonds are issued in increments of $1,000, $5,000, $10,000, $15,000, $100,000, and $1 million. The notes mature anywhere from two to ten years, and the bonds mature anywhere beyond ten years through thirty years. These types of bonds are attractive for all of the same reasons as T-bills: they're backed by the U.S. government, they're exempt from state taxes, and they're very liquid.

Corporate Bonds

Corporate bonds are backed by the company that issues them, so your money is as safe as the company issuing the bond. Keep in mind that to sell their bonds healthier companies don't need to offer as much interest as riskier companies. But before you buy any bond, check out the grade it has received from ratings firms such as Standard and Poor's (*www.standardandpoors.com*) or

Moody's (*www.moodys.com*). Most financial advisors and brokers will not buy corporate bonds for their clients that have less than an A– rating. The main agencies that determine credit ratings for corporate bonds are the above-mentioned Standard and Poor's and Moody's. The chart below shows their investment grade rating levels.

BOND RATINGS		
Standard & Poor's	**Moody's**	**Rating**
AAA	Aaa	**Investment Grade:** high quality, reliable, and lower yields (interest rates)
AA	Aa	
A	A	
BBB	Baa	
BB	Ba	**Junk Bonds:** lower quality, unreliable, and higher yields (interest rates)
B	B	
CCC↓	Caa↓	

Municipal Bonds

Also known as munis, municipal bonds are issued by local governments. These bonds offer the hard-to-beat bonus of being double tax-free, meaning the interest you earn from them is exempt from state and local taxes. Because of this exemption, they make great "cents/sense" for investors in high tax brackets. Tax-free munis pay lower interest rates than taxable bonds. So unless you rake in a lot of dough and can enjoy major tax savings, these bonds may not be appropriate for you.

The Inverted Relationship Between Interest Rates and Bond Prices

Most investors buy bonds for the income stream; they usually don't think about the bonds until they mature. There's nothing wrong with this approach, but be aware of your other options in case you hit an unexpected steep pitch on the money trail.

When you hold a bond to maturity, you will receive the full face value of your bond, meaning the total amount you paid for the bond, plus any interest due to you. If you decide to sell your bond before the maturity date, the market determines how much you will get for it.

Bond prices at any given time depend on current interest rate levels, which then help the market determine the supply and demand for bonds. The key concept to remember is that when interest rates go up, bond prices go down—and vice versa. The market value for a bond is the price, determined by supply and demand, you can get if you want to sell a bond in the marketplace before its maturity date.

Interest Rates Go Up ↑	=	Bond Prices Go Down ↓
Interest Rates Go Down ↓	=	Bond Prices Go Up ↑

Note: These corelations refer to a bond's market value only. If you hold your bond until maturity, you will get the full face value (the dollar amount imprinted on the face of the bond) for it.

Given the complexity of bonds, you may want to consider buying bond funds to achieve diversity within your portfolio of adventure backpack investments. Why? Well, bond funds are diversified; they own hundreds of different bonds within the fund that include taxable, nontaxable, high quality with low risk, and high yield with high risk (junk) bonds. No need for you to go calling the direct hotline to the U.S. Federal Reserve Board to buy one bond that will offer you minimal exposure to the bond market!

In addition, another advantage is that the initial minimum investment for a bond fund is normally much lower than for buying a single bond. Initial minimum investments are currently starting at $500. And if you like the idea of getting a payout from a bond twice a year, you will get this from a typical bond fund (that's why these types of funds are also called "income funds."). You can also arrange to get a payout from a bond fund every month if you like.

Bond funds are generally easier to deal with when it comes to investing in them and getting your money out of them, so they are what Wall Street calls a "liquid investment." Keep in mind, even if you don't need current income, these funds can help ensure that your portfolio is properly diversified.

Average Annual Return, 1980–2000	
High Yield Bond (Income Funds)	**9.52%** Average Annual Return
Source: Lipper Analytical Services	

The Stock Market

"You must take your chance."
—William Shakespeare

As with hiking, investing in the stock market involves occasional setbacks and difficult moments, but the overall efforts of the journey have proven worthy over time. Over the past two centuries, the stock market has produced an average annual rate of return of 10 percent. And since the 1980s stock prices have risen almost 15 percent a year. The market as measured by the Dow Jones Industrial Average, however, has fallen more than 20 percent during sixteen different periods in the twentieth century. On average, these periods of decline lasted less than two years, meaning, if you can stand a temporary setback over a few years, the stock market is a proven place to invest for the long term. All in all, the performance of the stock market is hard to beat. I suggest and would like to strongly emphasize that stock be your major long-term investment vehicle. Why? Because stocks have consistently outperformed other types of investments over the long haul, no matter what! Take a look at the chart on the following page.

Rock'em, Sock'em, Stock'em!

A stock is a piece of a publicly traded company (Wall Street refers to these as "equities" or "securities"). When companies "go public," they issue shares of stock that people like you and me are allowed to buy on major stock exchanges such as the

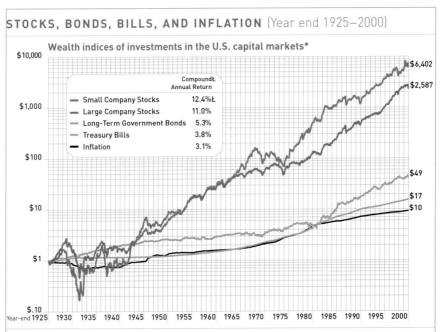

STOCKS, BONDS, BILLS, AND INFLATION (Year end 1925–2000)

Wealth indices of investments in the U.S. capital markets*

	Compound Annual Return
Small Company Stocks	12.4%
Large Company Stocks	11.0%
Long-Term Government Bonds	5.3%
Treasury Bills	3.8%
Inflation	3.1%

$10,000 — $6,402 — $2,587 — $49 — $17 — $10

Year-end 1925 1930 1935 1940 1945 1950 1955 1960 1965 1970 1975 1980 1985 1990 1995 2000

*Hypothetical value of $1 invested at year-end 1925; Assumes reinvestment of income and no transaction costs or taxes. This is for illustrative purposes only and not indicative of any investment. Past performance is no guarantee of future results.
Source: Ibbotson Associates, Inc.

NYSE (New York Stock Exchange), AMEX (American Stock Exchange), and the Nasdaq (National Association of Securities Dealers Automated Quotation System).

There are two ways to make money from owning a stock. One way is to have stock prices appreciate in value, as they generally do, as the economy grows and companies grow with it and earn more profits. The second way is through dividends. Dividends are how companies distribute a part of their profits to their shareholders. The two basic ways to invest in stocks are to

1. purchase individual stocks directly
2. invest in stocks through buying a mutual fund

The Skinny on Mutual Funds

A mutual fund is a professionally managed investment portfolio that offers individuals the ability to invest in a wide variety of shares. Each mutual fund seeks to meet the objective outlined in the fund's prospectus, which is sort of like a brochure without pictures. Regardless of how much you invest in a mutual fund, your piece of the pie is an exact replica of the entire pie, just a smaller version.

The reason you want to consider investing in a mutual fund is that as an investor, your goal is to put yourself first and to put away money each month to fund your adventure backpacks. You need to automatically stash away as much cash as you possibly can, and you can do this very easily with what is known as a systematic investment plan. This plan is an automated process by which your money market, checking, or savings account is debited (the norm is once a month) to fund an investment (typically a mutual fund) for one of your adventure backpacks.

Let's say that after gearing up budget lean and debt free you can save fifty bucks a month. This money now needs to go toward an investment. When you automatically put your money into a mutual fund each month, it will begin working for you immediately. Portfolio managers (trained professionals who decide what they are going to buy or sell with all the money the investors have deposited into the fund) will spend their entire workday investing your fifty bucks, along with a pool of money from other investors.

The financial management firms that hire portfolio money managers have the best available research tools and access to information that money can buy. Unless we are prepared to spend hundreds of dollars and unlimited amounts of time to become investment gurus ourselves, we should think of leaving the day-to-day of investing to a portfolio manager. You do want to have a life, right?

There are fifteen thousand mutual funds and counting. Many books have been written on "how to pick the right mutual fund for you." As this book is not dedicated to mutual fund investing, I will do my best to explain some of the basics about the different types of mutual funds available to you. But the reality is that you will probably need a financial professional to help you choose the right mutual funds for your adventure backpacks (I will discuss how to choose a financial professional later in this chapter).

Professional managers will argue about the quickest and safest route to wealth, but you need to decide for yourself which path you feel comfortable on. Depending on which mutual fund you choose, you can diversify a great deal here. Some mutual funds are made up of stocks that are only in the technology industry. Others are made up of just small, medium, or large companies, regardless of the industry. For example, here is a commonly used designation by size:

Small Capitalization =	the company is worth less than $1 billion
Medium Capitalization =	the company is worth between $1 billion and $5 billion
Large Capitalization =	the company is worth $5 billion and up

Mutual funds can be divided into two basic categories. Most are actively managed funds, which means portfolio managers use their own judgment to pick and choose the investments in the portfolio. The second type of mutual fund, an index fund, is passively managed. What is an index? An index tracks the performance of a specified group of stocks of companies large and small. For example, the Standard & Poor's 500 is an index that tracks the performance of five hundred companies. A typical index fund invests in nearly all of the stocks that make up a particular index and seeks to track the performance of that particular index. Because index funds are passively managed, they have cheaper expense ratios, which is what you pay to own the fund. Index funds are popular with many investors because they are inexpensive compared to managed funds and offer investors a way to track the performance of the different markets.

When it comes to actively managed mutual funds, you should think of packing your adventure backpacks with several different types.

Growth and Income Funds

These types of funds invest in companies, typically the nation's top corporations, that offer growth and income; their stocks are called "blue-chips." These companies normally produce revenues in excess of $1 billion a year, so they are medium or large-capitalization companies. These funds were created to offer investors a steady stream of dividend income accompanied with growth.

Average Annual Return, 1980–2000	
Growth and Income Funds	**14.35%** Average Annual Return
Source: Lipper Analytical Services	

Growth Funds

Growth funds invest mainly in growth stocks. These funds take a more aggressive approach that is designed to reap large returns over longer time periods. Growth funds make good long-term investments through focusing on capital gains, which is another word for growth, not dividends or income. Because of this strategy, they come with some risk. If you buy them, you should plan to hold them for at least a few years to take advantage of their strategy.

Average Annual Return, 1980–2000	
Growth Funds	**14.74%** Average Annual Return
Source: Lipper Analytical Services	

Balanced Funds

As the name implies, balanced funds take the middle path when it comes to risk and return. Balanced funds hold both stocks and bonds in order to secure growth without sacrificing principal. These types of funds are not as conservative as bond (income) funds, but they are also not as risky as growth funds, meaning your rate of return will usually be somewhere in the middle.

Average Annual Return, 1980–2000	
Balanced Funds	**12.89%** Average Annual Return
Source: Lipper Analytical Services	

Global and International Funds

Global and international funds buy investments from all over the world. The type of investments these funds make depends on the fund's objective: growth, income, balance, value, etcetera. Global and international funds offer you the ability to diversify your investments and participate in investment opportunities in foreign markets. The idea is to have approximately 10 percent exposure to these types of markets within your portfolio of adventure backpack investments.

Average Annual Return, 1980–2000	
Global Funds	**14.69%** Average Annual Return
International Funds	**12.2%** Average Annual Return
Source: Lipper Analytical Services	

Value Funds

Typically, value funds invest in undervalued companies of midcapitalization and large-capitalization companies. Portfolio managers of these funds look for companies that are down in price or undervalued. Think of it this way: it's like shopping only at the sale racks of your favorite stores. What's great about value funds is that if you shop around and pick the right type, you can get great return for low risk.

Average Annual Return, 1980–2000	
Large-Cap Value Funds	**14.85%** Average Annual Return
Midcap Value Funds	**12.28%** Average Annual Return
Small-Cap Value Funds	**12.91%** Average Annual Return
Source: Lipper Analytical Services	

Morningstar.com

As a retail investor, you can take advantage of a great option to research, review articles, and track the performance of the mutual fund universe. Morningstar.com offers unbiased, detailed information on an array of mutual funds, and the best part is it's free. All you need to do is log on to their Web site, *www.morningstar.com*, which is incredibly user-friendly for beginning investors, or call 312-696-6000.

Question Authority

Keep going! You're doing great! Now I'm going to take us one step further down the money trail. Most books on finance might stop right here when it comes to mutual funds, but I want you to take a deeper look into other exciting possibilities within the mutual fund investing arena. If you care this much to get started with your investing, odds are you care enough to want to know what you're investing in.

You know how shares of a public company work, but do you know what kinds of companies you're investing in? Would you want to know if you owned shares of a company that discriminated harshly against women or disobeyed child labor laws? Does a company hurt the environment or abuse animals? There's one way to find out.

Socially Responsible Investing (SRI)

What would you say if someone told you that the twenty in your pocket could bring you $4 just by packing it into a mutual fund every month? "Pretty cool," right? How about if someone told you that you could make good money with a mutual fund, plus effect positive change in society and the environment? What would you say? "No, thanks"? I don't think so!

In a 1999 Yankelovich study, 88 percent of women surveyed said, given the choice, they would select a socially responsible investment option. Why? It has been my experience that as women, we are consciously or subconsciously seeking to tap into something bigger than just making the grade.

During this "taking control" section of your money trail adventure, socially responsible investing is key. I believe that working off a healthy financial base is the first step on your amazing journey, a step that will help put into perspective every other aspect of your life. As your guide, I also want to share with you the awesome feeling of self-purpose you can get when you take the extra step into the philanthropic arena.

Socially responsible investing offers you the unique opportunity of making money and making a difference. Once you align yourself with your values through consciously choosing to invest in socially responsible mutual funds, you will see a distinct change in your outlook on life. No matter how awake we think we may be when it comes to social contributions in our own lives, we are really just sleepwalking if we aren't tapping into our community, our planet, and the type of social works we believe in.

So tell me more about socially responsible investing!

Well, if you don't know, you're far from being alone. Although socially responsible investing is experiencing a huge growth trend in the market today, not many people are aware of what it is. In fact, a Gallup Poll released May 16, 2000, stated that only one in four Americans investing in the stock market has heard of socially responsible investing, of which 27 percent claim to have money in such investments.

Socially responsible investing encourages businesses to address the specific challenges they may face on a social and environmental level. It's something I want you to know about because I'm glad someone told me. So tell me more, girlfriend!

In 1994 I was lucky enough to have exited stage left from the fashion industry and a somewhat sketchy six-year modeling career. I was offered a job in Hong Kong, where upon arrival I immediately began to pursue a fast-paced stock-brokerage career for four years.

I spent each year enthralled and consumed with myself, the markets, and making money. The island and "nature of the beast" of the Hong Kong community welcomed my selfish desires. I drank up my own rather large and unattractive ego each day when I stepped onto the dealing floor to trade out my clients' accounts. Colleagues who mirrored my desires surrounded me.

Self-consumption brought me nothing but a large pool of emptiness, however. If life was good and society was telling me I was successful, why was I feeling so terribly alone and lost?

> "When it gets dark enough,
> you can see the stars."
> —Charles A. Bears

Six months after my return to the United States a friend introduced me to socially responsible investing. I learned the basic concepts of socially responsible investing and was immediately hooked. I loved the idea behind it: making money while making a difference! I had the best of both worlds; I could pursue what I was good at, which was finance, but I could also be involved with effecting positive social change on some level in the world. That professional career change has continued to impact my daily life in positive ways.

> "Life, for all its agonies...is exciting and beautiful, amusing and artful and endearing...and whatever is to come after it— we shall not have this life again."
> —Rose Macaulay

Screening through SRI

Socially responsible investment houses, through their mutual funds and privately managed accounts, interact with publicly traded companies on behalf of their clients through screening. These funds first take into consideration the company's financial performance. After that, the fund performs company screenings to decide whether or not a specific company will be included in the fund's portfolio. A good example of this is the Women's Equity Mutual Fund, which monitors companies that present negative images of women and have histories of Equal Employment Opportunity Act violations, to make sure they are not included in their fund's portfolio.

Investors like us have myriad screening options available. If you are concerned about things like the environment, weapons, women's issues, human rights, animal welfare, or tobacco and gambling, an investment portfolio out there matches your concerns. And mutual funds like these are being introduced to the market on a regular basis.

Investors who use this screening practice are consciously putting their money to work in ways designed to achieve their financial goals while building a better, more humane economy.

"I have actually used the word *holistic*," says Barbara Krumsiek, president of the Calvert Group, one of the founding socially responsible investing houses in the country. "Everything is interrelated. The investment decision-making process is not separate from who I am as a person and how I make choices on a day-to-day basis," explains Barbara. "I'm going to make my investment decisions in a way that achieves my goals and in a way that reflects who I am as a person. You want to be able to meet that financial objective, but it's great to do so in a way that is consistent with who you are." Aligning your financial investments with your personal values can make for a very fruitful journey.

Shareholder Advocacy through SRI

Shareholder advocacy, on the other hand, is when certain funds approach a company with a movement for change. Managers of socially responsible funds serve as a voice for their investors, enabling them to "speak" to corporations. The managers submit and vote on proxy resolutions when companies refuse to talk or when the dialogue breaks down.

In the 1990s, shareholder advocacy, combined with other forms of activism, resulted in numerous success stories. Examples include Home Depot's decision to phase out its practice of buying old-growth timber by 2002, McDonald's decision to implement a sexual orientation nondiscrimination policy, and RJ Reynolds' decision to separate its tobacco business from its food business. And these guys are just the beginning. More companies are destined to live up to the challenging standards provided by socially responsible investing.

Just take a look at the fabulous socially responsible investing growth trends.

From 1995 to 2000, screened assets under professional management in the United States grew from $162 billion to a whopping $1.5 trillion. To give you a broader perspective, that's approximately 13 percent of all professionally managed funds in the United States. You could safely say that $1 out of every $8 is invested in some type of screened fund today.

These statistics show that screened investments, which are involved in shareholder advocacy, are likely to increase, in turn creating an even greater incentive for companies to pay attention to the concerns of socially aware investors.

This is great news, girls. It means we will continue to have more options for investing in a socially responsible way. You may be thinking, *How can I save the planet when, right now, I can't even save myself?*

When you take the time to go beyond "survival mode," which as young women we know all too well, and expand your mind's eye beyond your debt and your bills, you will be amazed at the sense of purpose and meaning life can offer you. It can give you a sense of connection, not isolation. Loneliness at times stems from the feeling of separateness. By connecting and giving back to society and the environment through socially responsible investing, you immediately tap into a feeling of unity. The best part about socially responsible investing is there's no need to compromise your returns to align with your values.

Your socially responsible fund doesn't have to suffer financial consequences for the positive social impact it will have. You can tap into this wonderful type of progressive investment tool without having to compromise your financial returns.

Eleven of the sixteen socially responsible mutual funds with $100 million plus in assets earned top performance marks in 1999 from two of the most popular mutual fund rating companies: Morningstar and Lipper. In addition, Morningstar notes that the socially responsible mutual funds it tracks are nearly twice as likely to receive a top rating of five stars as others in the general fund universe.

Where can I go for more information on socially responsible investing?

A couple of good spots that will help you get more familiar with the entire socially responsible investing concept and community include:

1. **The Social Investment Forum (SIF)** is a national non-profit membership organization promoting the concept, practice, and growth of socially responsible investing. SIF is the central hub for socially responsible investing. You will find a listing for all socially responsible funds, descriptions, and links. Check out SIF's Web site at *www.socialinvest.org* (202-872-5319).

2. **Socialfunds.com** has over a thousand pages of strategic content to help you make informed investment decisions regarding socially responsible investing. This fun Web site has a ton of great up-to-the-minute news on socially responsible investing. Check it out for yourself at *www.socialfunds.com* (802-348-7790).

3. **Green Money Journal** seeks to promote the awareness of socially and environmentally responsible business, investing, and consumer resources. Its goal is to educate and empower individuals and businesses to make informed financial decisions through aligning their corporate and financial principles. Contact them at *www.greenmoney.com* (509-328-1741).

Feeling confident? Feeling motivated? Good to hear. Now you're ready to make some more decisions.

Load and No-Load Mutual Funds

There are two basic types of mutual funds to choose from: load and no-load funds. Load funds charge you a set fee up front and/or upon redemption from the fund. The average load fee for mutual funds is approximately 5 percent. That means if you're looking to invest $100 in a load fund with a 5 percent up-front load charge, five bucks will be chewed up by the load charge and $95 will go toward your investment in the fund. The load fee you pay does not include the fund's expense ratio fee (total operating expenses of the fund that are passed on to the investor). Unlike a load fund, no-load funds do not charge you a set fee for investing in or redeeming shares from the funds. But just like a load fund, no-load funds charge you an expense ratio of approximately 1.5 percent. That means you will be charged each year you invest in a fund with an expense ratio of 1.5 percent, $1.50 for every $100 in the fund. As the cost of running the fund grows, so does the expense ratio.

Even though your inclination may be to collect no-load funds for your portfolio of adventure backpack investments, think again. You may need extra help choosing and managing your investments. Most load funds are offered through financial advisor guides. If you hire a financial advisor guide, she will be trained to help you achieve your goals and objectives. If you choose a fee-based financial advisor guide, which we will further discuss below, the annual cost to you is approximately 1.5 to 2.5 percent of the total value of your assets, including mutual fund fees. In short, packing load funds is not that much more expensive for you, approximately 1 percent extra, than packing no-load funds. The idea is that a good financial advisor guide should be able to make up the difference by offering you awesome investment advice.

TRAIL NOTES to Finding the Right Financial Advisor Guide for You

Studies have shown that we girls prefer to gather as much important information as possible before choosing any investment gear. In a study conducted by the University of California at Davis of thirty-five thousand financially savvy (meaning confident in their knowledge about investing) individuals, women investors outperformed men by an average of 1.4 percent per year. Why? Women aren't afraid to ask a financial advisor guide fifty questions before making an informed decision. On the other hand, men dislike admitting that they don't know (sound familiar, girlfriend?), hence, they only ask a financial professional guide about choosing investment gear and then *basta!* As a woman, you naturally have the upper hand when it comes to getting smart about choosing the right investment gear for your adventure backpacks.

Keep in mind, solid financial planning is not that complicated. It's all about knowing the right steps to take to the summit. I believe that we are all adventurous and capable young women. We could all choose to manage our investment gear on our own. However, I strongly suggest that before you make major decisions, get some advice from a financial advisor guide about the right steps for you. If you choose correctly, your financial advisor guide will make choosing your investment gear and managing your portfolio of adventure backpack investments much easier. Plus, she could possibly help you achieve greater results than if you tried to do it on your own.

Remember, we are young and have plenty of time to ride the waves of the stock market to make our money grow. Taking the time to talk with a financial advisor guide will help you trek to fantastic asset ascension on your money trail.

500,000 Financial Professional Guides and Counting...

If you believe that you may feel more comfortable about making your investment gear choices through working with a financial advisor guide, here's the 411. There are many different financial advisors out there, all qualified, with almost as many different titles to sort through, from financial planner to registered investment advisor, full-service broker, CFP (Certified Financial Planner), and CHP (Chartered Financial Planner). Ultimately, however, you want a financial advisor guide who can listen carefully to your money needs and goals and then offer you choices from the whole investment spectrum.

Financial advisor guides can be compensated several different ways. Traditionally they have been paid for their services through commissions, but now that commissions are getting smaller, most financial planners have turned to fee-based compensation. The annual cost to you to work with a financial professional is roughly 1.5 to 2.5 percent of the total value of your assets, including mutual fund fees. That means you're only paying an additional 0.5 to 1 percent—outside of no-load and load mutual fund expense ratios—to get informed advice that will enable you to make better choices with the investment gear available to you.

I appreciate that we all have different needs, but I believe that working with a financial professional who is compensated on a fee-based system vs. a commission-based system is better. There's no conflict of interest with a fee-based system. It's in the financial professional's best interest to make your money grow and not just flip trades to get a commission kickback fee.

Financial advisor guides can also charge for their services through consulting fees. And keep in mind that the financial services industry has been in a state of ongoing consolidation due to our wonderful friend the World Wide Web.

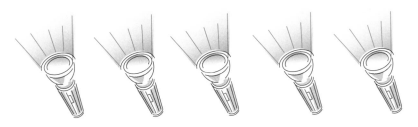

FLASHLIGHTS TO HELP YOU FIND A FINANCIAL ADVISOR GUIDE

FLASHLIGHT 1: Check out a potential financial advisor guide's history.

You need to make sure you can trust your financial advisor guide. After all, you're entrusting her or him with your very hard earned money. Many financial advisor guides, including me, were required to fill out what's called a U-4 form upon receiving their broker-dealer licensing from the NASD (National Association of Securities Dealers). The NASD keeps these forms on record for public viewing. Most top-tier finance firms will not hire a financial advisor who has a "shady" history. Therefore, you need to check out any prospective financial professional's U-4 form before you choose one. You can do this by telephone or by visiting the NASD Web site at *www.nasdr.com* (800-289-9999). Be sure to check the "Disclosure Events" file once you find your financial advisor guide's information page. This is where you will find legal dirt in their past, if there is any!

FLASHLIGHT 2: What can your financial advisor guide explain?

You want a financial advisor guide who can explain his or her investment views concisely and easily. Does he have a sound long-term plan? Experienced financial advisor guides will offer you their investment views, which they have carefully carved out over time through their experience and generally put to practice in managing their clients' money. You also need to make sure that the financial advisor guide you choose asks you detailed questions to get an in-depth understanding of your comfort level when it comes to risks. Your financial advisor guide should be able to calmly explain to you the risks associated with investing in each and every investment you choose together in the future.

FLASHLIGHT 3: Don't hire a financial advisor guide who brags about ascending the money trail in split seconds.

We young gals have been lucky to have lived in extremely robust economic times. The fact is that up until 2000, the domestic stock markets have been going gangbusters. As a result, it is easy for financial advisor guides to brag to you about double-digit or even 20 plus percent investment returns for their clients. Don't let this fool you! We've been in a technological revolution during the last six to seven years, and double-digit returns have been quite easy for a financial advisor guide or mutual fund company to come up with.

Remember earlier in the chapter when we chatted about the market over the past two centuries having an average rate of return of 10 percent? Well, any financial advisor guide who is going to brag about double-digit returns is not looking back far enough, like fifteen or even twenty years. Don't hire a bragger who is only going to give you a small window of time to talk about investment returns. The key to a great financial plan is to take the right steps. And make sure you step forward with someone who is using realistic projections based on more than the last five to ten years of investment returns.

After your first appointment with a prospective financial advisor, take time to be honest and examine your female intuition. This valuable compass will help steer you. Do you feel comfortable chatting with this person? Is this someone you think you could connect with and build a long-term professional working relationship with? Most important, is this someone you would want to trust your money with? Remember, just like credit card companies, there is an abundance of financial advisor guides out there for you to choose from.

FLASHLIGHT 4:
Be gracious.

You want your financial advisor to take note of you. She may have hundreds of clients, but your goal is to be remembered and to have her take note of you, regardless of the fact that you may only be holding a $2,000 Roth IRA with her. It's not just the amount of money your financial advisor guide manages for you that she may be thinking about; she will also take note of how you deal with her. A thank-you note or phone message can go a very long way! Make sure you set yourself apart from the herd and take the time, when appropriate, to thank her for helping you make money.

FLASHLIGHT 5: Make a pact with your financial advisor guide.

Draw up a checklist requesting the following from your financial advisor guide and have her review it and then sign it:

For the 1.5 to 2.5 percent fee you will pay your financial advisor guide request:

- that you receive a monthly statement from the brokerage firm that holds your money showing a detailed summary of all the current month's transactions, including deposits, withdrawals, and current positions held.

- that you get a detailed financial plan with an investment policy statement, or written agreement of understanding, that explains how your money will be invested. It should also highlight your goals and objectives.

- that she always get information you request on an investment and provide you with any questions you may have regarding that investment.

- that she explain in detail why she wants to make any new transaction in your account and explain all fees and commissions and that she give you a breakdown of all transaction costs, meaning the costs to buy and sell that should be included in the fee. And make sure to request that she return your calls in a timely manner!

- that you be kept informed about your money, and that if one of "your" stocks goes down dramatically, she call you to discuss it.

- that if she sells something that is in an account other than your retirement account, she first explains the full tax implications.

- that you receive from her a transaction slip from the brokerage firm that holds your money for each transaction she has made on your behalf.

- that she prepare and provide you with detailed quarterly and annual reports showing you the exact returns on your money plus all fees and commissions charged to you. Remember to make sure that the figure on her report matches what you received from your brokerage firm. These reports absolutely need to include all of the money you actually made or lost from selling an investment, otherwise known as the *realized* gains or losses, plus a breakdown of the investments you own but have not yet sold and thus that have not realized a profit or loss, otherwise known as the *unrealized* gains or losses. These quarterly and annual reports should also show you the performance of the market indexes for comparative analysis to your own returns.

In Wrapping Up

Use these five flashlights to help find the best financial advisor guide for you. I know this process may seem somewhat overwhelming at first and may even take a little while, but keep in mind that hiring a financial advisor guide will be one of the most important lifelong decisions you can make. If you choose to hire a financial advisor guide, make this decision a top priority. Make sure you take the time to interview several candidates, get references, and think your choice through carefully. You can do this! And think about how good you will feel once you have found the right financial advisor guide for you.

TRAIL NOTES on Asset Ascension through Asset Allocation

Before I take you through the trail notes on asset allocation, you need to begin to think of your three adventure backpacks as one big pizza pie that will make up your portfolio of investments. The percentage of pizza pie allocated to your emergency adventure backpack will be much less than for your retirement adventure backpack. And the portion for your dream adventure backpack will vary depending on how much it costs you to fund your dreams. Keep in mind that your retirement adventure backpack should always be the biggest slice of the pizza pie. After all, you will need to live off this for probably twenty or more years. Your emergency adventure backpack should end up over the longer term being the smallest piece of the pie. You only need to build up, max, three to six months of emergency reserved cash. And again, your dream adventure backpack will grow over time, so it will probably end up being the second biggest slice of the pie. But keep in mind, everyone's pizza pie will look different once it's sliced up. This is all about what works for you and what feels good to you. There is no right or wrong way to slice the pie as long as you make sure that your retirement adventure backpack garners the biggest portion.

Whether or not you choose to work with a financial advisor guide, you need to be familiar with the rough concepts of asset allocation, or deciding where your money goes. The idea of asset allocation is to help you capture the highest returns for the least amount of risk. How your money performs will always depend on the level of risk involved with whichever type of investment gear you choose. As you know by now, historically the returns on common stocks have exceeded the returns on bonds and money market instruments. However, in the short run, the values and returns on common stocks have tended to fluctuate wildly. By investing a percentage of your money in common stocks, bonds, money market funds, and other types of investments, you should be able to build more steadily your portfolio of adventure backpacks with a smooth return profile.

Making Math

The one broad-based school of thought when it comes to asset allocation uses a math equation involving your age and the level of risk tolerance you should think about adopting to determine how to spread your money around. Here's how it works:

Write your age down on a piece of paper. Subtract that from 110. The number you come out with is the percentage of assets you should put in stocks or stock-heavy mutual funds. Why? Because choosing investment gear that is heavily weighted with growth possibilities will offer you the best tools as young women to apex the long hike ahead of you. Plus, think about what your two best friends—time and compound interest—will do for you with great growth returns!

20 years old	30 years old	35 years old
90%	80%	75%

of your investments should be in stocks or stock-heavy mutual funds

What's left over can be put into bonds and cash investments. Remember, the stock market is going to be the best place for most of your investments if you are going to conquer the specific challenges we face as young women.

Key Notes to Keep in Mind

Creating and building your retirement adventure backpack is one of the best ways to ensure that you summit your money trail. Think of your retirement adventure backpack as a core piece of equipment for your long-term financial planning. Don't forget to put yourself first by stashing 10 percent of your gross income into your retirement adventure backpack before you dish out those hefty monthly expense checks to your landlord and credit card companies. When it comes to choosing savvy investment gear for your retirement adventure backpack, consider putting 90 percent or more of your investments in the stock market through direct purchase of stocks or mutual funds. As I discussed above, the stock market has produced an average annual rate of return of approximately 10 percent historically over two centuries (a 10 percent annual rate of return is good by general Wall Street investing standards). Remember, the key here for us hip hiker girls is time and compound interest. By choosing to have an asset-allocation model that exposes you heavily to the stock market, you are choosing investment gear that will help ensure your money grows in the best possible way. If this level of exposure and risk doesn't feel comfortable to you, however, consider investing 75 percent of your retirement adventure backpack in the stock market and the remainder in bonds.

Remember to fund your emergency adventure backpack with savvy investment gear such as money market checking accounts and/or CDs. Prepare yourself for the next crisis in your life by making sure you have a little short-term cash stash for the short-view hike. Last, take care to ponder what you would like to do with your dream adventure backpack. All you need to do to make your dreams a reality is identify what they are, decide if they are for the short or long term, and make a plan to finance them.

Ahhh! Take a deep breath. We're almost done. You, my friend, have conquered the hardest part of the journey. Congratulations!

Switchback Terrain

- There are several ways to to grow your money within your portfolio of adventure backpack investments. You will need to identify the best investment gear for you to pack into each of them.
- When hiking the money trail for the short view, you need to equip yourself with investment gear that is low risk and allows you to quickly access your money at any time along the way. The short-view hike has a duration time of one month to two years. Your investment gear options include
  1. money market accounts
  2. CDs
  3. U.S. Treasury bills

- When hiking for the long view, you need to equip yourself with investment gear that holds greater risk, thus offering you greater growth potential. Remember, when it comes to investing, risk and reward apex together. Your hiking duration for the long view will be anywhere from two to ten years or more. Your investment gear will include
  1. bonds
  2. stocks
  3. mutual funds
- During this "taking control" section of your adventure, socially responsible investing is an option worth knowing about. Socially responsible investing offers you the unique opportunity of making money and making a difference. Socially responsible investment houses, through their mutual funds and privately managed accounts, interact with publicly traded companies on behalf of their clients through screening or shareholder advocacy. If you are concerned about things like the environment, weapons, women's issues, human rights, animal welfare, or tobacco and gambling, there is an investment portfolio out there that matches your concerns.
- Studies have shown that women prefer to gather as much important information as possible through talking with a financial advisor guide before choosing any investment

gear. Use the "five flashlights" to help you identify the right financial guide for you. They are:

1. Check out a potential financial advisor guide's history.

2. Ask what your financial advisor guide can explain.

3. Don't hire a financial advisor guide who brags about ascending the money trail in split seconds.

4. Be gracious.

5. Make a pact with your financial advisor guide.

⦿ Whether you choose to work with a financial advisor guide or not, you need to be familiar with the rough concepts of asset allocation (deciding where your money goes). The idea of asset allocation is to help you capture the highest returns for the least amount of risk. How your money performs will always depend on the level of risk involved with whichever type of investment gear you choose.

chapter 6

Six Inspirational Summit Reserves

"This above all: to thine own self be true."
—William Shakespeare

Reserve 1: Keep it simple.

I am a daily practitioner of the popular ashtanga yoga practice. As an ashtanga yogini you are taught to keep it simple and that everything is meant to be, which means, don't make things in your life more complicated than they have to be. As a young woman you must always take the long view to secure your long-term financial future. Once you implement the concepts outlined in this book, the setbacks you have today or next month will not keep you from hiking for the long view on your money trail.

In order for you to build what is in your power to build, you must believe that everything that happens is positive. You may be thinking, *Vanessa, how can it be positive when I just split up*

with my college sweetheart and am not only suffering grief but am addressing money concerns? How can it be a positive thing if I didn't get the really great job that I wanted? Well, I am not trying to minimize the difficult feelings of disappointment, fear, worry, and pain these events might have triggered. In fact, I've been through these exact events myself. But the amazing thing I've learned is that if we choose to stay open, these events are truly gifts to us. Even when things seem unbearable, if you believe that somehow everything is happening for a reason that is ultimately for your benefit, especially when faced with the toughest challenges that life has to offer, you will have the ability to draw good out of any situation. You will be the type of person who can look for benefits, lessons, and growth opportunities in even the toughest situation. You will discover hidden treasures no matter what.

You never really know how things are going to end up happening until they happen. As they happen the way they are meant to happen, you will again see that everything is meant to be.

> "He who would have beautiful roses
> in his garden must have
> beautiful roses in his heart."
> **S. R. Hole**

Reserve 2:
Keep it clean.

By keeping it clean, you are also keeping it simple. How many of you are pack rats? Do you hang on to all of the latest *People* magazines just because Brad Pitt is on a few of the covers? How about your desk at work; is it organized? Can you find your stuff quickly and efficiently? Or is it filled with different papers, old coffee cups, and other miscellaneous items? Invest in yourself now! Take the time to clean up your act and stop wasting valuable time. Throw away old magazines, newspapers, or any other reading materials that you haven't read in the last thirty days. A clean, organized desk at work will show your boss and coworkers that you are on top of everything that's happening with your job—and your life.

Now move on to your home. Go through your closets, drawers (kitchen too!), and clothes—just get rid of whatever you don't use. Make a trip to the Salvation Army. Have respect for yourself, your financial life, where you live, and where you work by keeping it clean and organized. This inspirational summit reserve relates directly back to your first assignment in Chapter 1, when you organized your files. It also feeds into another crucial step you took in Chapter 3, being budget lean and debt free through uncovering and tracking the truth about where you really stand financially. Remember, you will have an immediate sense of control over your entire life if you keep it clean.

Reserve 3:
Embrace change.

Did you ever see the German movie *Run, Lola, Run?* You know, the chick with the flaming red hair? In the movie Lola has twenty minutes to come up with a large sum of money to save her boyfriend from being murdered by drug lords. The movie plays you three different scenarios of what Lola chooses to do in those twenty minutes to successfully save her boyfriend. What was most intriguing about this movie was how much everything changed with each scenario. Just like Lola, each one of us is consciously or unconsciously playing out different scenarios in our daily lives, some good and some not so good.

The idea is that we are all faced with challenges in this lifetime. But how we choose to respond to our challenges is the telltale sign of who we really are. Many of us believe we want a better job, more pay, cooler digs, a better partner, and so on, when, in truth, we can have whatever we want. But not if we are averse to change. Why? Because change is the key that will unlock the door for you to absolutely get what you want in this lifetime! If you are not changing, on some profound level you must ask yourself, "Am I truly living?" I understand that change is scary, uncomfortable, and at times extremely painful. But it is only when we practice believing in ourselves and in our dreams that we can really achieve what we want. And yes, sometimes the tunnel of change is very dark and makes you feel incredibly vulnerable and alone. But it has been my experience that the light always comes, and with it magical living.

If you are unhappy about your current financial condition—how much money you currently make or even how much credit card debt you have—no need to fear. Now is the time to take charge and make a plan for change. Start with one little positive step toward action and change today, and commit to another step each day going forward.

Do you want to live your life to the end with regrets? If you aren't risking and changing what you don't like today, will you be full of regret later? Now the question you need to answer is what do you want and are you willing to embrace change to get it?

> "Sometimes I go about pitying myself.
> And all the while I am being carried
> across the sky by beautiful clouds."
> —Ojibway Indian saying

Reserve 4:
Stand by your decisions.

This book is about taking charge, stepping forward, and making it all happen for wonderful you. Through embracing your financial future, you will empower yourself to live the quality of life you deserve. Remember, the only way you can move forward is by making decisions, *now*. I know how easy it is to waiver, especially if you are heavily PMS-ing! You tell yourself that you will wait till the next week, when you won't feel com-

pletely insane and hormonally out of whack. There are probably decisions about your professional, personal, and financial life
that you are putting off right now.

But you need to be proactive when it comes to making
decisions. Take the best information available to you at the time
and then make a decision based on that information. This
relates directly to finding a financial advisor guide, choosing
how to build your retirement adventure backpack, and even
deciding to get out of debt. Show self-respect and make sure
you follow through with owning your decisions.

Reserve 5:
Value yourself.

Each and every one of us is unique, which means each of us has
a special talent. It's up to us to discover *our* special talent. Have
you done that yet? Is there something that you absolutely love
to do? That's often an indication of a special talent. If you focus
on doing what you love to do, chances are you will be extremely good at it. Take the time to explore your thoughts and feelings when trying to figure out your special talent. While doing
this, you may even be able to come up with a few dreams to
include in your dream adventure backpack. By tapping into
your very own special talent, you are tapping into your flow.
And when you are "in your flow," you are setting yourself up
to reap wonderful benefits emotionally, spiritually, mentally,

physically, professionally, and financially. As the famous author Joseph Campbell has said, "It's up to each one of us to go into the woods and find our own path." What is your path?

Reserve 6:
Let it begin with you.

Use the tools I have offered you in this book as a call to action for yourself. Organize your financial information, create personal goals that reflect your true money values, be budget lean and debt free, build your adventure backpacks with savvy investment gear, and truly let it begin with you! Why? Because the only real control we have is over ourselves. If you spend a good deal of your time focusing on other people and what they are doing wrong, you're wasting energy. Focus instead on yourself and on addressing changes in your own financial life. True empowerment and consciousness begin with owning who you are, including your thoughts and actions. Let it begin with you! If there are things you don't like about someone or a situation, perhaps they don't need to change; perhaps you do. Remember, you can only change yourself and your own perspective. Don't give your power and energy away by focusing too much on what someone else needs to be doing. Begin with you and what you can do for yourself.

"The important thing is to not stop questioning."
—**Albert Einstein**

The End of Our Trail

We have reached the end of our trail together. May your financial future be filled with much light, love, laughter, and abundance. Keep in mind that a woman's experience isn't what happens to her, it's what she *does* with what happens to her. The life we choose to live is limited only by our imagination.

I hope you will take the lessons in this book and use them to help empower you to build the quality of life you want. Think beyond today and tomorrow to what you can create for your future—and then create it. All you need is the courage to head out on the money trail and incentive to do so right now.

INDEX

A

adventure backpacks
  asset allocation to, 169–170
  making best investments
    for, 173–174
  preparing/packing dream,
    128–131, 173
  preparing/packing emergency,
    104–113, 172–173
  preparing/packing retirement,
    113–128, 172
  summaries of, 132–133
  See also investments
Americorps, 99–100
AMEX (American Stock
  Exchange), 145
Angelou, Maya, 103
Apartment Lease Information
  file, 35
asset allocation
  to adventure backpacks, 169–170
  doing the math on, 171
ATM debit cards
  advantages of using, 90–92
  free with money market
    accounts, 106–107, 108
ATM withdrawals
  assessing/counting your, 74
  writing down/tracking, 80–81

B

Bears, Charles A., 154
The Bhagavad Gita, 93
"blue–chip" stocks, 148–149
bond prices, 142
bond ratings, 141
bonds
  "Bowie Bonds," 142

corporate, 140–141
  diversification through, 143
  municipal, 141
  Treasury notes and, 140
  types of, 139–140
Bowie, David, 142
Brown, James, 142
budget. *See* monthly budget
Bureau of Economic Analysis, 24

C

Calvert Group, 156
cash spending, 81
CDs (certificates of deposit), 137
Census Bureau, 14
CFP (Certified Financial
  Planner), 162
checking accounts
  money market accounts vs., 107
  organizing statements of, 34
  selecting interest for, 105–106
CHP (Chartered Financial
  Planner), 162
consumer prices (historical/
  projected), 21
consumption. *See* spending levels
credit card companies
  annual fees charged by, 87
  money-making strategies
    used by, 89
credit card debt
  assessing your, 83–84
  cash advances contributing to, 88
  compacting your, 84–87
  grace period of, 89
Credit Card Debt Information
  file, 34

credit cards
annual fees on, 87
cash advance privileges of, 88
keeping accurate information
on, 34
keeping limited number of, 81
minimum monthly balances
on, 88
secured, 88–89
seduction of, 82–83
Current Year Receipts Information
file, 35

D

debt
ATM debit cards to track, 90–92
credit card, 83–89
using Myvesta consultation to
control, 92
paying off highest interest
rate, 99
See also loans
defaulting student loans, 93–94
disability insurance, 108–109
Disability Insurance Services, 111
Disability Management
Sourcebook, 109
"Disclosure Events" file (NASD
Web site), 164
diversified investments, 135, 143
divorce
financial impact on women
by, 15–18
men vs. women's quality of life
after, 16
rates of U.S. (1920–2000), 15
Dow Jones Industrial Average, 144
dream adventure backpacks
elements of, 128–130

investment options for, 130–131
summary of, 133

E

earnings outlook projections, 28
Einstein, Albert, 27, 183
elderly women
impact of divorce on income
of, 15–18
statistics on income of,
11, 12–13, 14, 15
Elliot, Edwin, 59
emergency backpacks
bank accounts in, 105–106
disability insurance as part
of, 108–109
elements of, 104–105
money market accounts
in, 106–108
summary of, 132
Emerson, Ralph Waldo, 82
Employer-Sponsored Retirement
Plans
allowed contributions to, 117
early withdrawal/turnover
of, 120–121
401(k) plans as, 114–116, 117
403(b) plans as, 117
investing in company's
stock, 120
investment options of, 119–120
matching investment
into, 118–119
SIMPLE plan as, 117
types listed, 117
Equal Employment Opportunity
Act, 155
Excel, 76, 100

F

FDIC (Federal Deposit Insurance
    Corporation), 106
financial advisor flashlights
    being gracious to, 166–167
    cautions against bragger,
        165–166
    checking out history of, 164
    checking out investment views
        of, 164–165
    checklist for pact with, 167–168
financial advisors
    compensation paid, 163
    finding the right, 161–169, 175
    types of, 162
financial assessment checklist, 34–36
financial records checklist, 34–36
401(k) plans, 114–115
403(b) plans, 117

G

Gallup Poll (2000), 153
global and international funds, 150
Goethe, 121
Green Money Journal, 159
gross income, 78
growth funds, 149
growth and income funds, 148–149

H

Hepburn, Katherine, 42
Hoffman, Hans, 23
Hole, S. R., 178
Home Depot, 157
Home Mortgage Information
    file, 35

I

income
    earnings outlook projections, 28
    gross and net, 78
    impact of inflation on
        retirement, 22
    men vs. women's level of, 13–14
    Social Security, 18–20
    Social Security caps on, 18
    spending level vs., 22–25
    statistics on elderly single/
        widowed, 11, 12–13, 14, 15
    strategies on keeping your, 26
    See also money supply; personal
        finances; spending levels
individual pre–tax retirement
    accounts
        IRAs/Roth IRAs, 122–125
        SEP IRAs, 125–126
        types of, 121
inflation
    as investment challenge, 20–22
    stocks, bonds, bills and, 145
    Institute for Women's Policy
        Research, 14
insurance
    additional individual, 110–113
    disability, 108–109
    record keeping/information
        on, 35
Insurance Information file, 35
interest rates
    bond prices and, 142
    for checking/saving accounts,
        105–106
    comparing credit card to
        savings, 86

credit card debt and, 84–87
paying off credit with highest, 99
refinancing loans with lower, 95
investment gear
    long view, 138–143
    short view, 136–138
investments
    asset allocation and, 169–170,
        171
    average growth rate of, 33
    bonds, 139–143
    dedication of millionaires to, 29
    diversifying your, 135, 143
    gathering statements on, 35
    "latte factor" of, 32
    mental foundation of, 31–32
    mutual funds, 146–151
    prioritizing opportunities
        for, 30–31
    selecting your best options
        for, 173–174
    short-term/long-term, 136–143
    SRI (socially responsible
        investing), 152–159
    stock market, 144–145
    time advantage of, 32–33
    See also adventure backpacks
IRAs (individual retirement
    accounts), 122–125
Iron Maiden, 142
IRS Web site, 99

J

Johnson, Samuel, 10
Johnson, Scott, 36
Jung, Carl, 135

K

Keller, Helen, 73
Kennedy, John F., 74
Kgositsile, Keorapetse, 5
Krumsick, Barbara, 156

L

large capitalization designation, 147
"latte factor," 32
Liabilities Information file, 35
Lifetime Learning Credit, 99
Lipper, 158
load mutual funds, 160–161
loans
    consolidating/refinancing/
        prepaying your, 94–95
    Sallie Mae administration of
        student, 96–98
    trail notes on student, 93–94, 95
    See also debt
long-term goals, 66–67
long-term investments
    bonds as, 139–140
    described, 138–139

M

Macaulay, Rose, 155
McDonald's, 157
Mandela, Nelson, 7
medium capitalization designation,
    147
men
    investment performance of
        women vs., 161
    postdivorce quality of life of, 16
    poverty rates of women vs.,
        17–18
    retirement benefits/income of
        elderly, 14, 15

unequal pay/retirement benefits
of women vs., 13–14
Merrill Lynch, 16
Microsoft Excel, 76, 100
mid-term goals, 66–67
The Millionaire Next Door
(Stanley), 28
miscellaneous expenses assessment,
72–73
money market accounts
checking accounts vs., 107
in emergency backpacks,
106–108
as short-term investments, 136
money supply
assessing your budget and, 75–78
managing your, 74–75
miscellaneous expenses impact
on, 72–73
trail notes on controlling your,
78–82
See also income; spending levels
money supply adventure backpacks
asset allocation to, 169–170
making best investments
for, 173–174
preparing/packing dream,
128–131, 173
preparing/packing emergency,
104–113, 172–173
preparing/packing retirement,
113–128, 172
summaries of, 132–133
money trail
getting on the, 2–3
hitting the, 9–10
specific hurdles faced by women
on, 37
summit checkpoints on, 22–39

summiting the, 4–5
summit reserves on, 177–183
See also personal finances
money trail challenges
inflation as, 20–22
Social Security blues as, 18–20
summary of, 37–38
you are trekking solo, 14–18
money values
assessing compatibility of goals
and, 63–64
assessing spending in terms of,
52–53
examples of women's, 43–47
family influence on personal,
47–49
impact on financial plan by,
41–43
incompatibility of lifestyle
and, 47
listing your own, 58
list of sample, 57
matching lifestyle choices
with, 50–56
summary of, 68
See also value-packed goals
monthly budget
example of average, 77
financial information confirmed
by, 77–78
keeping a, 76
nonlimiting budget plan for, 79
summary of tips on, 100–101
trail notes on controlling
your, 78–82
See also spending levels
Moody's, 141
Morningstar.com, 151, 158
municipal bonds (munis), 141

mutual funds
    balanced, 149–150
    global and international, 150
    growth, 149
    growth and income, 148–149
    Lipper ratings of, 158
    load and no-load, 160–161
    Morningstar.com ratings
        on, 151, 158
    overview of, 146–148
    value, 150–151
Myvesta, 92

N

Nasdaq
    combined composite index,
        23–24
    stock exchanges on the, 145
NASD (National Association of
    Securities Dealers), 164
National Center for Women and
    Retirement Research, 16, 18
National Council of Women's
    Organizations, 12, 13
net income, 78
no-load mutual funds, 160–161
nonlimiting budget plan, 79
Nonqualified Information file, 35
Norman, Marsha, 130
NYSE (New York Stock
    Exchange), 145

O

Onassis, Jacqueline Kennedy, 59
"Overview of the Economy"
    report (Bureau of Economic
    Analysis), 24
Owner's OCC coverage, 113

P

"Paying Yourself First" plan,
    113–114
Personal Earnings and Benefit
    Statement (Social Security), 19
personal finances
    assessing miscellaneous expenses
        and, 72–73
    checklist for assessing, 34–36
    first step to security/
        independence in, 7–8
    first step toward independence
        of, 7–8
    value–packed goals as tools
        in, 41–43
    values related to, 41–42
    See also asset allocation; income
pre–tax retirement accounts
    compounding interest
        of, 115–116
    Employer–Sponsored
        Retirement Plans, 116–121
    401(k) plans, 114–116
    individual types of, 121–126
    overview of, 114–116
    three investing steps for, 127
    trail tale on investment options
        of, 127–128
Publication 970, 99

R

Retirement Accounts Information
    file, 35
retirement adventure backpacks
    "Paying Yourself First" plan
        for, 113–114
    pre–tax retirement accounts
        for, 114–128
    summary of, 132

retirement income
  of elderly single/widowed
    female, 11, 12–13, 14, 15
  impact of inflation on, 22
  impact of spending level on, 25
  men vs. women's, 14
RJ Reynolds, 157
Roger, Diane, 65
Roosevelt, Theodore, 30
Roth IRAs (individual retirement
  accounts), 122–125
Run, Lola, Run (film), 180

S

Sallie Mae, 96–98
savings accounts
  organizing statements of, 34
  selecting interest for, 105–106
Schultz, Howard, 63
secured credit cards, 88–89
SEP (Simplified Employee Pension
  Plan) IRAs, 125–126
Seymour, Jane, 41
Shain, Merie, 49
Shakespeare, William, 3, 144, 177
Sharpe, Sandra, 131
short-term goals, 65, 66–67
short-term investments
  CDs (certificates of deposit), 137
  money market accounts, 136
  Treasury bills (T-bills), 137–138
SIF (Social Investment Forum), 159
SIMPLE plan, 117
small capitalization designation, 147
Socialfunds.com, 159
Social Security
  gathering account information,
    19, 34
  retirement income from, 18–20

Social Security Administration's
  Web site, 19
spending levels
  as challenge to creating wealth,
    22–23
  assessed in terms of money value
    of, 52–53
  ATM debit cards to track, 90–92
  miscellaneous expenses portion
    of, 72–73
  of millionaires, 28–30
  paying with cash to control, 81
  statistics on American, 23–25
  stopping the cycle of rising,
    23, 25–27
  tracking your, 80–81
  trail notes on cutting back,
    78–82
  See also monthly budget
SRI (socially responsible investing)
  importance of, 152–155
  information sources on, 159
  screening investment using,
    155–156
  shareholder advocacy through,
    156–159
Standard and Poor's, 140, 141, 148
Stanley, Tom, 28, 29
stock market, 144–145
student educational programs
  Americorps, 99–100
  Lifetime Learning Credit and, 99
student loans
  paying back, 93–94, 95
  Sallie Mae and Dept. of
    Education administration of,
    96–98
Summers, Vanessa
  all about, 1
  financial "awakening" by, 11–12

financial education/experience of, 1–2

on the money trail, 2–3

setting value-packed goals, 60–61

summit checkpoints
    available investing opportunities, 30–37
    income/spending/wealth connection, 22–30
    summary of, 38–39

summit reserves
    embrace change, 180–181
    keep it clean, 179
    keep it simple, 177–178
    let it begin with you, 183
    stand by your decisions, 181–182
    value yourself, 182–183

T

taxes
    defaulted student loans and refunds from, 94
    income before and after, 78
    Lifetime Learning Credit toward, 99
    municipal bonds and, 141
    pre-tax retirement accounts and, 114–128

tax return records, 36

Tax Returns Information file, 36

Third Millennium survey (1994), 19–20

Thoreau, Henry David, 28, 55

Tillich, Paul, 56

Treasury bills (T-bills), 137–138

Treasury notes, 140

U

U-4 form, 164

Ullman, Samuel, 71

Unum Provident, 111

USAA Insurance, 111

U.S. Commerce Department's Census Bureau, 14, 17–18

U.S. Department of Education, 94, 96

U.S. Securities and Exchange Commission, 106

Ustinov, Peter, 75

Utilities Information file, 35

V

value funds, 150–151

value-packed goals
    example of young women's, 43–47
    family influence on personal, 47–49
    as financial plan tools, 41–43
    gathering together, 59–64
    incompatibility of lifestyle and, 47
    matching lifestyle choices with, 50–56
    sample of short-term/mid-term/long-term, 65–67
    setting time checkpoints for assessing, 64–65
    summary of, 68–69
    See also money values

value-packed goal trail notes
    assessing value/goals compatibility, 63–64
    detailing goals, 64–66

reviewing your goals, 61–62
sharing your goals, 62–63
summary of, 69
writing goals down, 59–60

W

Web sites
Americorps, 100
credit card rate information on, 84
for disability insurances, 111
IRS, 99
Moody's, 141
Morningstar.com, 151
Myvesta, 92
NASD, 164
Sallie Mae, 96
Social Security Administration, 19
on SRI information, 159
Standard and Poor's, 140
U.S. Department of Education, 96
women
disabilities claims by, 110

financial impact of divorce on, 15–18
financial statistics on working, 8–9
investment performance of men vs., 161
poverty rates of men vs., 17–18
retail therapy indulged by, 27
specific hurdles faced by, 37
statistics on elderly single/ widowed, 11, 12–13, 14, 15
unequal pay/retirement benefits of, 13–14
Women's Equity Mutual Fund, 155
Women's Institute for a Secure Retirement, 13

Y

Yankelovich study (1999), 152
Yutang, Liu, 54

Z

Zadra, Dan, 62

About Bloomberg

Bloomberg L.P., founded in 1981, is a global information services, news, and media company. Headquartered in New York, the company has nine sales offices, two data centers, and 79 news bureaus worldwide.

Bloomberg, serving customers in 100 countries around the world, holds a unique position within the financial services industry by providing an unparalleled range of features in a single package known as the BLOOMBERG PROFESSIONAL™ service. By addressing the demand for investment performance and efficiency through an exceptional combination of information, analytic, electronic trading, and Straight Through Processing tools, Bloomberg has built a worldwide customer base of corporations, issuers, financial intermediaries, and institutional investors.

BLOOMBERG NEWS℠, founded in 1990, provides stories and columns on business, general news, politics, and sports to leading newspapers and magazines throughout the world. BLOOMBERG TELEVISION®, a 24-hour business and financial news network, is produced and distributed globally in seven different languages. Bloomberg Radio™ is an international radio network anchored by flagship station BLOOMBERG® WBBR 1130 in New York.

In addition to the BLOOMBERG PRESS® line of books, Bloomberg publishes *BLOOMBERG® MARKETS, BLOOMBERG*

PERSONAL FINANCE™, and *BLOOMBERG*® *WEALTH MANAGER*. To learn more about Bloomberg, call a sales representative at:

Frankfurt:	49-69-92041-200	São Paulo:	5511-3048-4530
Hong Kong:	85-2-2977-6600	Singapore:	65-212-1200
London:	44-20-7330-7500	Sydney:	61-2-9777-8601
New York:	1-212-318-2200	Tokyo:	81-3-3201-8950
San Francisco:	1-415-912-2980		

About the Author

Vanessa Summers is a registered investment advisor with the Department of Corporations in the state of California. Her professional life began as a fashion model in New York City, with the Ford Model Agency representing her during the beginning of her career. At age twenty-three she went on to become a sales trader in Hong Kong with Jardine Fleming, a top-tier brokerage firm, and then moved back to the United States in 1998 to become the Head of Sales and Marketing for a women's fund. In the beginning of 2000, out of a deep desire and passion to help other young women conquer their own money trail, Summers founded and currently serves as Chief Adventure Officer of the Sutra Foundation, an educational-based nonprofit that seeks to motivate, inspire, and educate young women to get started with investing and planning for financial retirement. Its mission is to foster empowerment for young women through financial education. The author's interests include hiking, biking, kayaking, sailing, snowboarding, watching sunsets, laughing, socially responsible investing, and keeping an adventurous perspective on life with her many amazing friends. Her friends describe her as fun, energetic, and outgoing, qualities she attributes to her daily ashtanga yoga practice. Summers divides her time between San Francisco, California, and Jackson Hole, Wyoming.

About the Sutra Foundation

The Sutra Foundation, established in the spring of 2000 by the author Vanessa Summers, is an educational-based nonprofit organization that seeks to motivate, inspire, and educate young women to get started with investing and planning for financial retirement. Summers has assigned and directed that all advances, royalties, and other payments earned on her behalf for writing *Get in the Game! The Girls' Guide to Money and Investing* be donated to the foundation to help further its mission. The first two publicly recognized projects of the Sutra Foundation have included a groundbreaking work of research on "Young Women (ages 21—34): Thoughts, Attitudes, and Behaviors about Money and Investing," released in spring 2001 and co-produced with Third Millennium, the leading advocate for young people on Social Security reform, and Oppenheimer Funds, one of Wall Street's leading advocates for women; along with publication of *Get in the Game! The Girls' Guide to Money and Investing*.

The foundation's board members are all dynamic women who seek to support an extensive outreach and call to action for young women around the country to get in the game (and get out of debt), to take control of their financial futures, and in return offer themselves

empowerment through financial education!

According to the Institute for Women's Policy Research, approximately 50 percent of all elderly (sixty-five and older) single/widowed women live on incomes of less than $12,000 per year. It is the passion of Vanessa Summers and the Sutra Foundation's board members to ensure that all young women have been informed of the woeful financial condition of too many elderly women in this country and offered educational information on how to start taking control of their personal finances now.

How You Can Help

The Sutra Foundation has implemented a call-to-action out-reach program to help fulfill its "Empowerment Through Financial Education"–based mission. The program calls for

- companies to work with the foundation on a strategic sponsorship basis, to jointly create awareness of the need for young women to begin saving and investing, through educational projects such as workshops and seminars for young female employees and nonemployees, events and conferences, and other types of projects.
- companies and individuals to volunteer their time and professional expertise.
- companies and individuals to donate monies directly to the foundation.

To Learn More

To learn how corporations and individuals may make a fully tax-deductible contribution to the Sutra Foundation in support of its programs and activities, you may contact the foundation or visit its Web site listed below. Please include your contact details and e-mail address if you would like to receive via e-mail the Sutra Foundation newsletter, "Call to Action Update."

The Sutra Foundation
2280 Green Street, Suite 301
San Francisco, California 94123
Web site: *www.sutrafoundation.com*
E-mail: vanessa@sutrafoundation.com

You may also log on to *www.sutrafoundation/getinthegame.com* to access more information about this book directly from the author, Vanessa Summers.